THE
TRUST TRIFECTA

A Leader's Guide to Hitting the Trust Jackpot

THE
TRUST TRIFECTA

A Leader's Guide to Hitting the Trust Jackpot

JORDAN BERMAN

IGUANA

Editor: Toby Keymer
Front cover design: Meghan Behse

ISBN 978-1-77180-420-2 (paperback)
ISBN 978-1-77180-421-9 (epub)
ISBN 978-1-77180-422-6 (Kindle)

This is an original print edition of *The Trust Trifecta: A Leader's Guide to
Hitting the Trust Jackpot.*

TABLE OF CONTENTS

This is for my children.
Anything is possible.
Even writing a book.

Part One

SETTING THE CONTEXT

MEET JUSTIN RAY

*"The single biggest problem in communication is
the illusion that it has taken place."*
— *George Bernard Shaw*

Justin Ray sat quietly. He watched his boss's lips move but just couldn't seem to process the information. "I recognize this is difficult to hear Justin, but we are not including you on the succession slate for the CEO role at this time," Joanna said. Joanna was the current CEO, and had been playing an active role in the plans to replace her when she retired in the next three years.

It was Justin's first performance review in his new role as Executive Vice-President, Marketing, and he had a difficult time reconciling what he was told by Joanna with the feedback he had received throughout his career. He'd always been a top performer and considered a "HiPo" (HR speak for "high potential") who could essentially do no wrong.

While intuitively Justin knew he had shortcomings, they had never seemed to hold him back from consistently being promoted to increasingly senior roles. Sure, over the years he had been given feedback about how he interacted with others, so Joanna's feedback wasn't about a total lack of self-awareness. But only now, in this specific moment, did he realize that he'd never applied the feedback he'd been given and that it had finally caught up to him, as it does with everyone.

He felt completely deflated. During his two years with this company, he had exceeded his objectives — launching new products, surpassing sales forecasts, maximizing revenue from his existing portfolio, and winning awards for the creative he and his team developed. In all his one-to-one meetings and performance discussions with his manager, nothing was ever shared that suggested Justin's plan to be considered CEO-potential was remotely coming off the rails.

However, according to Joanna and the stakeholders she had consulted for feedback, Justin was not a "strong leader." Yes, he delivered results. But he struggled to get others to support him and trust him, including members of his own team.

Some of the stakeholder comments Joanna received referenced Justin holding onto information instead of sharing it. Others shared that he frequently did not provide enough context for decisions that he made. He came across as evasive when people asked tough questions, and he could be curt in his communication when under pressure.

Finally, while Justin perceived himself as a loyal employee committed to the company's values, and reminded his team of their importance, he was not seen as modelling the values himself. Essentially, even if he was a strong communicator, it didn't matter because his actions did not support his words.

His direct reports almost always "fell in line" and delivered his agenda, but not without considerable resistance, distraction and, for some, plain old disengagement. They just didn't feel connected to him. One team member left the company about six months after Justin became their manager. In their exit interview, they told HR that they didn't think Justin "had their back."

Even though his credentials and his "what" weren't in question, his "how" was. This dichotomy seemed to emerge as an epiphany for Justin during his review. On his way back to his office after the meeting with Joanna, Justin reflected further on what he had heard. And in these few moments of unfiltered honesty with himself, memories of interactions and exchanges with colleagues came flooding back to him where he recognized he could have done better.

Meet Alison Davis

"People will forget what you said, people will forget what you did, but people will never forget how you made them feel."

— *Maya Angelou*

"Thank you for your guidance, Alison, it means a lot to me," said Mike Beytel as he left her office. This was Alison's first general management role: her many years in progressively senior roles had taken her all the way to the top. She had been Aztec's President and CEO for almost two years now.

However, it wasn't just that Alison had steadily climbed the venerable "corporate ladder" to reach the prestigious corner office, or that she achieved this at a time when female leaders continue to face challenges getting promoted, it was *how* she climbed it. Throughout her career, she had always focused on creating strong connections with those around her because of *how* she led, not *what* she achieved. She created this same experience with everyone she worked with, whether they were direct reports, peers, or people senior to her. Alison had achieved her success in large part because she recognized early on that leadership is all about getting stuff done with the support of others. And that support comes when people trust you.

To her credit, she also possessed strong self-awareness and was not just open to feedback from performance reviews, but also made a concerted effort to apply it. Though the feedback had sometimes been difficult to hear, she was fortunate that her managers and stakeholders were transparent in sharing it.

Some of her most valuable feedback came early in her career from a future mentor who told her: "The most important thing you can do as a leader is to create trust with the people you work with." This had always resonated with Alison and she kept this advice front and centre as she grew and developed as a professional. She also recognized that her role as a leader wasn't about her: it was about being in service to others. Alison readily admits that she has always strived to maintain that mindset so that she creates the most value and benefit for those she leads.

Clearly, this approach had worked, because it was Alison's "how" that had elevated her to the role of President & CEO. Even though she had been missing some of the key experiences and achievements (the "what") the recruiter and employer were looking for, she had excelled at relationship-building — a clear marker of cultivating trust — demonstrated by the fact that she had a long track record of people who followed her from role to role as she advanced in her career. Her ability to make strong, lasting connections and to build trust were the difference makers for the decision makers at Aztec.

THE WHAT & THE HOW

"The first job of any leader is to inspire trust."
— *Stephen M. R. Covey*

I have worked with and provided counsel to hundreds of Justins and Alisons over the past 30 years. I have seen trust fostered and I have seen it eroded. I've witnessed leaders who were remarkable in their style of engaging and mobilizing others. I have also seen leaders who were considered rock star performers on the achievement side (the "what") but who ignored the "how" side and suffered as a result, even if it took some time. I have experienced the profound impact a highly trusted leader can create for employees and indeed, an entire organization. Unfortunately, I have also experienced the opposite.

My goal in writing this book is to share insights from working with both types of these leaders so that you can strengthen your own leadership. The take-aways in this book can be immediately applied and are relevant for both established leaders who may be stalled in their careers but are looking for advancement, and new leaders charting their own paths. This book is a unique road map and approach to trust-building that *works*.

So let's begin with a broad yet fundamental question: What kind of leader are you?

Are you more similar to Justin or Alison? Be honest.

Are you the kind of leader who has developed meaningful relationships with those around you? The type of leader who is intentionally focused on *how* stuff gets done as much as *what* gets done? The kind of leader who takes a back seat and empowers those around them to realize their full potential? Or maybe you're the type of leader who, having reached the perceived pinnacle of success in the hierarchy of professional life, assumes it's because of your competence and achievements? Is that you?

Perhaps you are a blend of both Justin and Alison.

One thing is clear: of the countless definitions of leadership that float to the surface in a simple Google search, the more common definitions all include references to the "what" of leadership (a.k.a. competence):

- Setting a vision
- Mobilizing people to buy in
- Setting goals
- Building alignment
- Developing and executing a strategy

They are achievement focused and very much about the key activities a leader must perform effectively. There's no doubt the "what" element of leadership is critical for success. There is indeed a lot of "what" to do every day for someone leading a team, department, function, or entire organization.

But just as critical is *how* leaders go about delivering the *what*, as Justin found out (rather late in his career). This is frequently under-emphasized as a factor in someone's performance, in part because we are a very goal-oriented culture. There are, however, signs of hope. In fact, over the past ten years, particularly in corporate settings, *how* employees deliver their performance has gained increasing recognition.

Johnson & Johnson (J&J) for example, a company that is almost 135 years old, modified its performance management process to account for the "how" only in the past decade. Today at J&J, an employee's performance review includes equal weighting for both the "what" — did an employee achieve their individual performance objectives? — and the "how" — by what means did they achieve said objectives? The "how" is typically evaluated by the demonstration of company values and behaviours.

This shift in thinking from the "what" to the "how" is at the core of this book. More specifically, it focuses on the "how" to help you elevate your leadership ability using a blend of compelling, powerful, and impactful communication to build connections, trust, and followership.

WHY IS THE "HOW" SO IMPORTANT?

Connections are critical because to get stuff done as a leader you need to engage others. To achieve this, you need trust. Trust is the fuel for the "how" and is the most important element of leadership, bar none.

However, too often trust is equated with competence. It's assumed that because a leader has demonstrated that they can "lead" (a.k.a. "get stuff done"), people must trust them. This is a foundational assumption that has significant and wide-ranging ramifications when left unchecked. It disrupts the basic dynamic between leaders and others and, as a result, will eventually set all leaders up for some type of failure or setback. This may not always be immediately recognized, remember Justin? But the fact remains — if competent leaders fail to build trust then:

- How can you expect to mobilize others to buy into your vision?
- How can you build alignment around a set of goals or a strategy such that everyone moves in the same direction?
- How can you manage to get a single person, let alone dozens, hundreds, thousands, or hundreds of thousands of people, to implement your plans?

In short, without connections and therefore trust, how do you expect to deliver all of your "what"? People trust others for all types of reasons, and these are important to understand:

1. People trust you when they feel they "know" you.
2. People trust you when they feel you are being "straight" with them (a.k.a. being truthful).

3. People trust you when they see you talking and behaving in a consistent manner.

Notice anything similar about the above statements? They either contain the word "feel" or refer to perceptions. That's because connections (of which trust is the foundation) are about what people experience when they interact with you, listen to you, and follow you. And the most effective way to connect with others? Consistent, transparent, and authentic communication. Enter the Trust Trifecta©.

THE TRUST TRIFECTA

The Trust Trifecta© is a powerful way of communicating based on an intentional, mindful, straightforward approach. When the three elements — communicating consistently, transparently and authentically — are combined, they become an unstoppable force for deep connections and trust-building.

In horse racing, a "trifecta" is a bet that predicts which horses will place first, second and third in exact order. Similarly, there is a pecking order in the Trust Trifecta in terms of which communication principle is considered the most valued (i.e. which comes in first place). Using the analogy of a race, authenticity places first, transparency a close second, and consistency third. All very important, but a clear winner in the most coveted position.

If this seems like a simple concept, that's because it is. Build connections using impactful communication so that people will trust you. Once they trust you, they will follow you. And once you have followership, then you can deliver on the "what" that is expected of you as a leader.

The Trust Trifecta is not only based on my personal experience: it is also based on data, including the feedback of hundreds of thousands of employees via engagement surveys at companies I have worked with or provided counsel to over the past few decades.

The principles of the Trust Trifecta are also backed by an abundance of research. One such study, called the CanTrust Index, is the most in-depth study of Canadians' trust levels. In its 2019 report, when respondents were asked which leadership traits are the strongest drivers of trust, they ranked transparency and authenticity in the top five (with number one and two being honesty and integrity, both of which are closely linked to transparency). The report also concluded that "leadership [that] openly communicates and is accessible" was a critical organizational action in determining how much people trust an organization. It placed a close second, with 70% of respondents saying this.[i]

But a concept being simple doesn't mean that implementing it successfully is also simple. There are many reasons effective leadership communication can be challenging, and these are important to understand if you are committed to improving your skills in this area. The first, and perhaps most obvious, challenge is that it just isn't a priority for most people. Like anything else in your world, until it becomes a priority, it won't get the time and attention it requires (and deserves!).

Understanding why it isn't a priority for most people is also important. If you are a newly minted leader, for example, you are most likely focusing all your energy and efforts on delivering quick wins to demonstrate your value. True? That's understandable. But as you begin to transition into your new role, team, or department, and begin to build those connections and relationships, be conscious of the role that communication plays and how you "show up" in interactions with all your new stakeholders. It can be a real game changer.

What about if you are an "established" leader? How much time do you set aside to honestly think about building trust or using effective communications skills?

In my experience working in privately owned companies, multinational conglomerates, and smaller not-for-profit organizations, there are many reasons why people are promoted to leadership roles, and their ability to communicate with impact and to foster trust often *isn't* typically one of them.

This occurs because of the simple yet faulty formula surrounding competence. Here is the formula:

Leaders move into leadership roles because they are largely seen as competent. If you are competent you must have strong communication skills. Once you are promoted, the very act of promotion serves to validate that assumption for you. And when that happens, you don't see the value in developing this skill because it hasn't hampered your career advancement to date. Just wash, rinse, repeat what you have done before and success will follow.

Except when it doesn't. Remember Justin Ray?

Without self-awareness, skill development, and candid feedback during performance reviews, this cycle of unintended reinforcement of leadership by the notion that "competence trumps all" only serves to derail leaders as they progress through their careers. But this cycle can be broken, and, as a leader, you can have an active role in breaking it.

As a supportive manager who gives feedback, you can create meaningful, long-lasting relationships. The fact that Alison received this type of candid feedback and guidance from her managers throughout her career is evidence of this benefit. And the fact that many people have followed her from role to role as she progressed is a concrete example of the impact of connection-building through effective communication. Yet despite the clear benefits of this, trust-building remains off the radar for many leaders.

Best-selling author and well-respected thought leader on the subject of trust, Stephen Covey, along with Doug Conant, former CEO of the Campbell Soup Company, have reinforced that for leaders, trust-building often takes a back seat. Their joint Harvard Business Review article on "The Connection Between Employee Trust and Financial Performance" concluded that "while few leaders would argue against the idea that trust is necessary for building elite performance, not nearly enough realize the height of its importance and far too many disregard trust-building as a 'soft' or 'secondary' competency."[ii]

What I find perplexing about this is that the repercussions from a lack of trust are so obvious.

Think about it this way. If you had a leader who had demonstrated competence but was a poor communicator, in that they were inconsistent, were not transparent, and lacked authenticity, would they be able to build connections and trust on competence alone? I can't see how.

However, if you had a leader who used the Trust Trifecta to their advantage even in the absence of competence, could they build connections? Absolutely. We see it time and time again with leaders in business, sports, politics, and many other arenas.

The goal of this book is for you to better understand the importance of trust-building, the profound impact of connections, and how to build these connections in a meaningful and sustainable way. It challenges the notion that competence reigns above all else as the most important leadership attribute and elevates communication to a position of greater influence for leaders seeking the holy grail of leadership: followership.

Part Two

GOING DEEPER

AND THE RESEARCH SAYS?

"After all, the ultimate goal of all research is not objectivity, but truth."

Helen Deutsch

The importance of trust-building through communications seems obvious on the surface. However, this isn't just an observation, it's a fact based on considerable research that demonstrates the hard truth about the "soft skill" of communications.

The fact is, regardless of the size of your organization, high levels of trust deliver better organizational performance. Here are a few powerful research outcomes:

- Towers Watson, a multinational risk management, insurance brokerage, and advisory company, reported a strong correlation between effective communication and strong performance — that is, organizations that are highly effective at communications are nearly twice as likely to financially outperform their competitors as those who aren't effective.[iii]

- In another study, Towers Watson found that companies with highly effective communications had 47% higher total returns to shareholders during the previous five years compared to those with the least effective communications. They also found that companies that communicate effectively have a 19% higher market premium than companies that do not.[iv] Many other organizations have also fielded studies on this subject that share similar conclusions.

- In terms of trust and its impact on performance, Watson Wyatt, a global consulting firm, conducted a survey with close to 13,000 workers across all industries that showed that high-trust organizations had a total return to shareholders (stock price plus dividends) that was 286% higher than low-trust organizations.[v]

It's also worth noting that the value of trust is more than one-way. That is, while most studies tend to examine the impact of employees' trust in management, there are also studies which explore the implications when employees feel trusted *by* management.

In one such study, authors Sabrina Deutsch-Salamon and Sandra L. Robinson showed that employees who felt trusted by their organization became more willing to accept responsibility for their organization's performance.[vi]

Would it seem such a stretch then to also suggest that if employees feel more responsibility for their organization's performance, they are also likely to work harder, smarter, and more efficiently in order to contribute to higher performance?

IN THE ABSENCE OF TRUST, COMPANIES SUFFER

Another way of examining the importance of trust is to consider the implications of not only having it but losing it. These can range from an unexpected turnover in employees to the creation of stronger silos in an organization. Consider each of these implications on its own.

Take increased turnover. There are tangible costs to replacing employees who leave an organization. These can include recruitment fees which can be substantial, especially for roles vacated at the senior levels within a company or organization. There is the associated disruption in this scenario if there isn't a clear and ready-to-implement succession plan for these roles.

There is the time and effort spent on finding new employees, from developing job posts and conducting interviews, to preparing job offers and conducting background checks. Then there is the lost time in productivity when the new employee begins because of onboarding and training. None of these "downstream" implications are typically considered linked to the broader impact of trust-building and trust-erosion.

Consider something even less obvious than the two outcomes highlighted above: reputational issues. If the person or people who leave an organization share the reasons for their departure with their network (e.g., "it's a terrible culture because the leaders can't be trusted"), and those people then share it with their network, this can create a negative profile for an organization. And the downstream implication of this could be, of course, challenges with recruiting new employees.

Then there are the more "hidden" impacts of low-trust culture. What about siloed thinking and behaviour that can result from lost trust? Do companies that suffer from this experience any negative consequences? Yes. Not only can low trust negatively impact employee engagement (a key contributor to organizational performance), but a lack of collaboration that results from this can ironically lead to a further strengthening or entrenchment of silos, causing a misalignment of priorities, inefficiencies due to duplicated efforts and, lost business opportunities.

Finally, there is the impact that a lack of trust has on the culture of an organization. Think about how much time and energy is devoted to hallway or water cooler talk when trust is eroded. How do you think this affects productivity and engagement (again, both markers of performance)?

TRUST CAN MAKE BRANDS SOAR

If you want to consider performance on a different level, think about Jack Welch and Oprah Winfrey. These are two very different leaders who were and are highly trusted in their given fields. Between them, they cultivated followership in the tens of millions of people.

These "followers," most of whom never met or interacted with either Welch or Winfrey, placed such trust in the words these leaders have shared that they have altered the way they operate their own businesses and, in Oprah's case, even the way they live their lives.

So how did each go about building such deep trust?

In his book *Winning*, former General Electric boss Jack Welch wrote as one of his eight rules of leadership: "Trust happens when leaders are transparent, candid, and keep their word." This sounds a lot like Alison's communication style.[vii]

He decries situations where leaders hoard information that could benefit direct reports in the performance of their duties. This, he says, drains trust right out of a team. This, as you'll recall, was one of the pieces of feedback given to Justin over the years.

In his two decades at the helm of General Electric, Jack helped grow revenues to $130 billion from $25 billion and profit to $15 billion from $1.5 billion. Pretty consistent.

Among his eight rules of leadership, competence isn't mentioned once.

Oprah Winfrey is an American media mogul, TV host, actress, producer, and philanthropist. She is also one of the richest and most powerful American women. One of her hallmark traits is a deeply sincere, authentic, and informal manner that has helped connect her followers with her and, ultimately, her brand. This is reflected in the following (candid) quote from her: "I had no idea that being your authentic self could make me as rich as I've become. If I had, I'd have done it a lot earlier."[viii]

Is Oprah competent? Of course. But her ability to build a global brand wasn't based on her playing the competence card with her television viewers. She didn't trot out an academic degree that said, "you should listen to what I say and take my advice because I went to school and know what I'm talking about." She was just being herself and communicating in a consistent, transparent, and authentic manner. These have been the hallmarks of her personal brand from the outset, and the key to her phenomenal success.

Despite these and many other examples, as well as a vast array of studies on the subject, strong communication capabilities continue to be in short supply. LinkedIn, the popular business networking app, conducted a recent US study seeking insight on the most coveted "soft skills." At the top of the list? Communication.[ix]

KEY TAKEAWAYS

- Communication is a key driver of high-trust organizations.
- When used effectively, communication can increase employee engagement, which is linked with stronger financial performance.
- A lack of trust can negatively impact an organization's culture in a concrete way.
- Low-trust cultures can lead to unexpected turnover, difficulty recruiting new employees, time and energy expended in recruitment, onboarding and training, increased silo building, and a lack of alignment around company objectives.

BATTLE OF THE Cs

"Success demands a high level of logistical and
organizational competence."

— *George S. Patton*

Twenty-two pages in and I'm hoping you've bought into the idea that trust is a difference maker in leadership and organizational performance. I also hope I've made the case for why communication trumps competence in building that trust, and the value of building up your communication skills. However, if you are still wavering, I'm going to share a piece of research and a well-known case study to get you over the finish line. First, the research.

The relationship between competence and communication was highlighted in a 2018 study published in MIT Sloan Management Review, where researchers sought to examine "why people believe their leaders — or not."

Using a nine-point scale, the researchers asked 145 employees in a range of organizations to rate leadership behaviours as indicators of competence and trustworthiness — traits that people associate with credibility. What they found was that effective communication was in the top five behaviours for leaders who were viewed as competent. They also found that communication played a similar role when leaders were viewed as trustworthy, with "communicates openly with others" in the top five behaviours.[x]

Yet time and again, competence is highlighted as the key to success when communication plays a critical role. That's why I love the quote from Patton above. It reinforces the commonly made assertion that competence equals success. Interestingly, a quick search on the hallmarks of successful military teams lists more references to the need for unparalleled trust and effective communication than it does competence.

However, just as Patton asserts above in relation to the battlefield (by focusing on the "what"), the same holds true in boardrooms around the world, where discussions regarding talent management (and promotions) take place. "Let's review what Sarah or Jim has accomplished." But the tide is slowly turning, and not just among HR professionals who frequently drive talent discussions within companies.

David Solomon, CEO of Goldman Sachs, remarked when discussing leadership, "The other thing I'd point to is that there is a real emphasis when people are interviewing around academics and I.Q. I think it's way over-weighted. There should be equal emphasis on E.Q. and how you interact with people, how you relate to people, and how you connect with people."[xi]

This point is also underscored by the now-historic 2016 US election. In that showdown, you had a political novice and reality television star face off against one of the most competent opponents in US history, Hillary Clinton, and what happened? Competence was swept to the sidelines, while Trump built trust through impactful communication.

Obviously, there were a myriad of factors that contributed to Clinton's loss. Indeed, many were outside of her control. But it's undeniable that her inability to connect with voters played a pivotal role. It always does in election campaigns. Beyond the policy platforms, a candidate's values and vision, and frustration and anger that may exist among the electorate, the ability to connect with voters is critical.

If you consider the election through the competence lens, this point becomes even more pronounced. Clinton had been a Secretary of State for four years, a US senator for eight years, and the First Lady for eight years. Not a bad CV. But was her competence enough to sway voters and serve as a catalyst for trust? No. Nor was her ability, or lack thereof, to communicate consistently, transparently, and authentically.

In fact, in reviewing the endless analysis on why Clinton lost you can clearly see that trust was a key factor. One year before the election, Politico published an article reinforcing this idea with the headline "Can Hillary overcome the "liar" factor?" The article was based on a Quinnipiac University poll held in the fall of 2017 that showed more than three-in-five voters, or 61%, thought Clinton wasn't honest and trustworthy.[xii]

Some of the facts cited from the poll included what Politico termed "indictments" of her trustworthiness, including descriptors from poll respondents such as "liar," "dishonest," and "untrustworthy." "In an era of declining confidence in government, it's not unusual that voters would find a politician less than honest. But the striking reality is that, for Clinton, a lack of trust is the first thing many think of," Politico went on to say.

Clinton knew she had the upper hand in the arena of competence and perhaps even recognized or accepted that voters didn't trust her. This strategy was reflected less than three months before the election by the *New York Times* in an article titled "Hillary Clinton Asks Not for Trust, but for Faith in Her Competence."[xiii] The competence card was meant to turn the tables given her track record of experience versus her opponent. However, we know from the election results that this card was not enough to form a winning hand.

The dynamic between competence and communication as fundamental sources for trust-building is further affected by other "Cs" as well. These include credentials, character, and credibility, a few additional attributes of leadership.

SEIZE THE Cs

CREDENTIALS

Years ago, I was working with an organization that was transitioning from one President to another. Employees were asked to gather in the atrium to hear a few words from the incoming President. She was polished, articulate, and clearly competent based on her remarks and an overview of her credentials given by the current President. But minutes after she stepped away from the microphone, I heard the following comment from someone standing just behind me: "I don't trust her."

How is it possible that within minutes of hearing a stranger deliver a few complimentary yet very general comments, people already felt that she wasn't trustworthy?

It's because trust evokes something visceral within us, something instinctual. It's simply a feeling. And some people just *felt* they couldn't trust her. It wasn't the "what" (either what she said or what was said about her), it was the "how" (how she delivered her message). But she was polished, articulate and almost flawless in her remarks. So, what gives?

This example provides a powerful reminder that employees aren't looking for perfection in their leaders. This is a common assumption that leaders have about the need to communicate without error. Certainly, polished speakers can be impressive and may leave a memorable impact, but *polish* doesn't translate into *connection*. In fact, "perfect" communication breeds suspicion and erodes trust because it chokes out the chance for authenticity to surface.

Thus, as counterintuitive as it may sound, imperfect communication is much more powerful at creating connections and trust than communication that is error-free.

This isn't to suggest that the two are mutually exclusive. You can be both polished and articulate, but to build connections, you may also need to consider dialling up some of the communications fundamentals such as tone, body language, and pace.

If you're sitting there thinking that the employee who made the comment rushed to an early judgment of the new President, I can understand that. But what you and I think is irrelevant. It's not about us. The reality is, leaders often forget this. They underestimate the impact of what they say and how they say it. And let's face it, as a leader you are judged to a very high standard. Employees often hang on your every word, especially during times of transition or challenge. Without even intending to, employees will look for the most subtle nuances in your language, tone, and delivery, and rightly or wrongly conclude meaning from these. Fair or not, that's reality. So yes, you do always need to be "on."

You may also be sitting there thinking that building trust takes time. I agree. But you also know what they say about first impressions — they are powerful and difficult to change.

Perhaps this new President did spend some time thinking about the impression she wanted to leave with the hundreds of employees she would be leading. But what are the chances she thought to herself the following: *The best outcome from my two-minute remarks would be if people left feeling like they could trust me. And if that's the goal, what are my options for building that trust in such a short window of time?* Or, do you think it's more likely that what went through her mind was something like: *I need to seem like a leader who is up to the job — knowledgeable, confident, and articulate.* The truth is, neither of us know for sure, but I would bet every dollar I have that consciously or not, her goal leaned toward the second approach.

Contrast this with Alison from the beginning of the book. In her first address at Aztec, she said this: "Good afternoon. I admit that when I was told I only had two minutes to address you, I felt a bit overwhelmed (authenticity). There is so much I want to say about what I believe we can accomplish together, but I will need your help [transparency]. As we get to know one another, please be generous with your experiences here at Aztec, what's working well, and importantly, what can work better. I really look forward to getting to know you, learning from you, and working with you. Thank you."

Alison was just as deliberate about planning her meetings with direct reports. They weren't rushed or formulaic: she spent whatever time was necessary to demonstrate that each employee mattered. She shared information about herself, her past successes and failures, and this helped foster connections.

The incoming President I referenced above had never learned this skill and it was obvious in every interaction. She was all business, all the time. As a result, she just couldn't connect with people. She shared virtually no personal information and never engaged in the most basic conversational exchanges about trivial subjects (e.g., how her weekend was, or whether she did anything interesting on her vacation).

Instead, she emphasized her competence at every turn. She always had the "right" answer even when there was more than one possible answer. In fact, even when challenged by others who were considered experts on a topic, she would frequently disagree with them and claim they were wrong.

Despite receiving candid feedback about how she communicated and "landed" with others, she could not adapt in a way that enabled connection. Thus, even with her impressive academic and business credentials, as well as the endorsements from other respected leaders, trust simply evaded her. As Will Rogers said, "You never get a second chance to make a great first impression." She lasted in the role for less than two years.

CHARACTER

Character is another attribute that can be either amplified by effective communication or derailed by it. For example, you can't say one thing and then turn around and behave in a manner inconsistent with your words. If you do, it cuts right to the core of your character and leaves this question in people's minds: *Can I trust this person?* That's because in part character includes the foundational trait of integrity, and integrity is inexplicably linked with trust because it is also interconnected with honesty. There is no better way to reflect this link than from the well-known quote from author C. S. Lewis: "Integrity is doing the right thing, even when no one is watching."

At the same time, a person's character also shows up when people *are watching,* and this is often seen in their behaviour but also in how they communicate. This is probably the reason why when you search the term "character traits" on the internet, "good communicator" is almost always in the list.

Character is powerful because it is what distinguishes us as individuals. It shapes our behaviour and reflects who we are as our most authentic selves. It is deep-seated and encompasses our set of values and beliefs.

If you look at character through the lens of the Trust Trifecta, it's clear how our values and beliefs influence our communication style. Integrity = transparency. Empathy = authenticity. What about consistency?

Psychologist Sherrie Campbell wrote an article for *Entrepreneur* magazine in which she shared "seven character traits exceptional leaders have in common." What topped her list? "Possess high levels of self-control." She went on to share that such leaders "see no point in overreacting or allowing their emotions to dictate their words…" I would build on her position and reinforce that it is not just about the words, but again, how those words are shared, which can be especially difficult when someone feels under pressure.

For example, I was working with a very senior executive several years ago on an extremely important document that would provide direction to a global organization on how they would succeed moving forward. High-stakes work no doubt. However, while me and others who were working with this leader were looking for calm and clear direction and communications from this leader, what we would frequently experience, often within the same business day, was constantly changing direction from her on how to proceed. This inconsistency borne out of an emotionally charged situation, only served to create confusion, frustration, and low morale among the team who felt we couldn't do anything right.

CREDIBILITY

Credibility is in the same category as character and credentials because it also drives trust. As with the other Cs, credibility should be considered part of the price of entry. That is, it's probably stating the obvious (but here I am stating it anyway) that we tend to follow people who are credible in what they say. We do this because at the core of credibility is truthfulness, and we tend to follow people who satisfy our appetite for truth.

To boost your credibility when communicating, you must at a minimum be consistent. However, there are several other strategies for enhancing your credibility. Try referencing third parties such as think tanks or leaders from other companies or sectors. One easy reference point is the industry association of your sector. Although it may be considered less credible because of its shared interests with your organization, it does elevate facts beyond simply internal claims.

While facts, stats, and studies can be important in helping to validate your message, you must use them prudently to avoid diminishing emotional impact (the connection-building part of your message). Too much data, and this gets lost.

The most impactful aspect of strengthening your credibility is knowing your content. This may seem obvious, but many leaders I've worked with don't spend the time required to really internalize their messages, and as a result it impacts both the credibility of what they're saying and their ability to be authentic in saying it.

It may seem counterintuitive to suggest that you internalize your content to the point where it comes across as authentic. That's because for some people, authenticity is equated with "speaking off the cuff." I'm not in that camp.

By "owning" your message, you will inevitably be much more comfortable in communicating it, and when that happens, it lands in a credible and authentic way. The audience is more apt to believe what you are saying because it's clear that you believe what you are saying. This is markedly different from a leader who speaks to a group of employees and has "learned" (insert "memorize" here) a set of key messages. When this approach is taken, it just comes across as scripted and ends up hurting your character and credibility (as well as parts of the Trust Trifecta such as transparency and authenticity). In short, being prepared and being authentic are not mutually exclusive.

If we revisit the familiar ground of politics, we see this all the time. Political leaders frequently struggle with balancing the need to "stay on message" while simultaneously avoiding coming across as a programmed robot. In Clinton's case, she was deemed not to be credible precisely because she was deemed to lack transparency, honesty, and therefore trustworthiness. This was in part because of *how* she communicated, not just *what* she said.

After a politician speaks about something of "importance" (defined only by the fact that the media is reporting on it), a panel of pundits will frequently analyze their performance in terms of whether that politician "stayed on message" or "went off script." I'm convinced if these politicians spent more time internalizing the essence of their message instead of simply remembering the words on the page (or the teleprompter), the pundits and analysts would be starved of fodder to dissect.

Barack Obama was an anomaly to this frequently used "stay on message" approach when speaking. When fielding questions, whether it was at a press briefing or a town hall, his cadence and thoughtfulness before responding to questions enabled him to convey a clear position that was aligned with his policy direction without sounding "messaged." He was a leader who effectively utilized character and credibility to his advantage.

One of the best strategies for tackling challenges that may arise with establishing credibility comes from Jeff Ansell, author of *When the Headline Is You*. He advises leaders to "acknowledge scepticism to boost credibility."[xiv] What Ansell is highlighting is the value of parking your ego and allowing others to have a different point of view from yours. This is a powerful concept that helps increase credibility, because people tend to find a person — especially a leader in an organization — more credible when that leader seems open to viewpoints other than their own. In other words, don't be defensive: resist the urge with all your strength!

To effectively respond to someone who is questioning your credibility (or the credibility of your facts, etc.), just accept it and meet them where they are intellectually. You can do this easily by simply saying: "I can appreciate why that might cross your mind" or "I understand why you could come to that conclusion."

Unsurprisingly, this approach is not only disarming, but also reinforces the principle of transparency because it shows you understand and appreciate that not everyone is on board with a position, direction, or information that is being shared.

KEY TAKEAWAYS

- Competence has been (and continues to be in some lagging organizations) the traditional "go-to evidence" when discussions take place about who should be promoted to a leadership role.
- The Three Cs, credentials, character, and credibility, are critical contributing factors in the formula for building trust and are closely linked to, and influenced by, the principles of the Trust Trifecta.
- Credibility can be enhanced by supporting your position or argument by citing third party facts, positions, and statistics.
- Be careful about how much you rely on facts and stats, as you don't want to dilute the emotional impact of your message — being able to tap into emotions facilitates powerful connections.
- Being an authentic communicator does not mean speaking "off the cuff." By owning and internalizing your content, you will be able to convey it more conversationally and therefore authentically.

Part Three

THE TRUST TRIFECTA©
IN ACTION

CONSISTENCY IS CRITICAL

"Trust is built with consistency"

— *Lincoln Chafee*

Consistency is one of those concepts that can evoke a big yawn. Consistency isn't sexy. It's inherently predictable. Who's getting revved up about a leader being consistent? But consistency is one of the keys to using communication effectively to build trust.

Consistency is challenging. It requires what I refer to as the "new R & D" — rigor and discipline. Being rigorous and disciplined can be difficult, especially when it comes to something we've done our whole lives (communication): we do it without much thought or intention. It's also difficult if we never pause to reflect on how we connect with others through our communication. We take for granted that it occurs because as "leaders" we have somehow demonstrated this ability, so we don't need to make it an area of focus.

The other challenge that consistency faces is that it is frequently misunderstood. This is particularly true in the business context. Consistency is so much more than simply repeating the same message over and over again. Done right, consistency is about conveying a message *and an experience*, words *and actions*, in a unified way. You simply cannot say one thing and then behave in a manner that is incongruent with your words. This is one area where Justin missed the mark as a leader. He frequently did what was expected of him, but this did not line up with either what or how he communicated or behaved with his team.

Reflecting on his conversation with Joanna after he left her office, Justin recalled how on more than one occasion he was guilty of upsetting the "consistency harmony" — backing up words with supporting actions. He gave himself a pat on the back that at least a few times he "said the right things" to his team, but his follow-up actions didn't support his words. It was like for the first time a light went off and he suddenly understood how his inconsistent behaviour had compromised his credibility, and as a result his ability to build trust.

What is noteworthy about consistency (as with the other two principles from the Trust Trifecta) is that it seems so obvious. Of course, we should be consistent in what we say and what we do! Similarly, of course we should be honest (transparent) and genuine (authentic) when we communicate. But intellectually appreciating that something is "obvious" and making it a reality are two different matters altogether.

Another obstacle of communicating consistently is that we frequently operate in dynamic environments. This means that a number of factors can impact what we say at any given time. These factors can include verbal or written commitments such as budget changes, unexpected leadership exits or changes, or a myriad of other unanticipated issues that will inevitably demand some type of communication. If you work in a global organization, there is also direction from global head office, which can impact local plans and decisions that you might have already made and communicated in your local market.

The best way to overcome this obstacle is to rely more heavily on the other principles of the Trust Trifecta — transparency and authenticity. Being upfront with your stakeholders when something has changed from what you previously had communicated and providing ample context for the change in direction (or its timing, or whatever is relevant) will almost certainly garner you some forgiveness and support. What does this look like in practice? "I realize last time we were together, I informed you about topic X.

Since that time, here is what has happened that has changed the course of that decision." Context is always essential in impactful communication.

PLAN FOR CONSISTENCY

Notwithstanding the fact that "things change," which can compromise what has been communicated, one of the more effective ways to stay on a consistent path with communication is by thinking ahead. You need to plan for consistency and to anticipate whether the commitments, statements, and observations you share could be nullified in the short term. You should always be considering a longer-term perspective where possible and what could be communicated in the coming weeks or months to ensure you remain consistent with what you say on any given day. In some cases, decisions can be made that do not align with what you have communicated. In others, decisions that were made may be changed. In either scenario you need to pivot. Take advantage of the pivot and frame it in a positive way. For example, "our ability to revisit a decision shows our courage" (or agility, or whatever value or skill it's relevant to highlight).

Here's a familiar example of something I have lived through many times over the years:

Company A announces that it will be restructuring its business. The senior management schedules a town hall to share the news. A few weeks later the affected employees leave the organization. Within days, the impact of the restructuring is still alive and well in the organization and anxiety manifests itself in people's minds in the most obvious way: *Will there be more job cuts?*

This topic and related questions emerge at almost every turn as employees seek employment security. So how should you answer this question? What if there might be some additional headcount reductions, but that decision has yet to be finalized?

What if you haven't been informed by senior management about the next steps yet? Perhaps even senior management doesn't know when this might occur: it could be three months from now, or not for another year.

An easy and credible way to help ensure you don't box yourself in with statements you may make is to qualify your statements by avoiding "absolutes." Absolutes refer to statements such as "we will" or "we won't." Words such as "never" and "always" are also ones to watch out for. Remember, if there is even one time when your statement doesn't hold true, your consistency will suffer, as will your credibility and transparency. Good qualifying statements that allow you to communicate honestly and with integrity include:

- "At this point in time…"
- "What I can share with you today is…"
- "I won't say never…but what I can tell you is…"

Communicate honestly and with integrity while avoiding the inclusion of any firm commitments or statements (e.g. we will always, we will never). Importantly, these statements are also credible and transparent. You are communicating what you know and don't know at a given point in time.

That said, there are a few occasions when the use of "always" is acceptable or warranted, such as: "We will always endeavour to share with you everything we know as soon as a decision has been finalized" or "We will always make the health and safety of our employees our first priority." There is a place for "always" and "never," but that place and use should be selective. Again, as a leader, you should always (there is another approved use of the word!) strive for a balance of honesty and integrity in your communication.

One common scenario where I've seen opportunities for more consistent communication is at the conclusion of a senior leadership offsite. These are typically important planning meetings and are frequently visible to others. They may even be part of a formal annual business planning process as an enterprise or a department within the company. It's likely that employees (or at least the direct reports of those at the offsite) are aware that an offsite is occurring, so it's important for meeting participants to be prepared to speak to it when returning to the office.

To ensure consistency, participants should discuss and align on — or be told, if it is a larger group — what can or should be disclosed about the content discussed at the offsite. Be explicit about it: send the messages in writing after discussing it with attendees. Use rigor and discipline (the new R&D) to help reinforce consistency.

In the absence of this, the result could be a number of different storylines making the rounds at your office. Agreeing on the messages up front eliminates the risk of participants having different interpretations about what was discussed, what should be shared, when it should be shared, and how it should be framed. No doubt you have witnessed this in your organization. People leave the same meeting where the same content was communicated to everyone in the room. Then somehow, almost mysteriously, various versions of that content begin to trickle into the organization as if through a game of broken telephone. Comments, decisions, statements, and actions get mixed up and make it a near impossibility that you will be able to convey a consistent narrative. In fact, a more likely outcome is that without a coordinated approach to messaging, a rumour mill might be accidentally started.

Another key aspect of planning for consistency is to ensure that you link messages with previous messages. This is particularly important if you want to ensure an ongoing focus on key areas. For example, perhaps you have made a major decision and communicated effectively. Coming back to that decision when future milestones or major accomplishments are delivered is what will enable employees to hear a familiar narrative. Here is a hypothetical example to illustrate this concept: The leader of a department communicates a new organizational model, which is designed to accelerate decision making by flattening the hierarchy in the team. The goal is to drive accountability down further into the organization and heighten empowerment at the more junior levels of the team. Once it has been announced, the leader should look for opportunities that demonstrate the goal of this change and explicitly link it back to the original decision. For example: "Earlier today we successfully outbid our most important competitor because we were able to turn around the data package and response to the request for proposal very quickly. Our agility signaled to our new customer our ability to be nimble despite our large size."

CONSISTENCY UNDER PRESSURE

Of course, the criticality of consistency is only amplified when the stakes are high. Being consistent during times of challenge can be particularly difficult, but keeping your message focused is of paramount importance. One such example of a focused message was shared in the well-known annual Edelman Trust Barometer from the global PR agency Edelman.

In discussing aspects of this barometer, Edelman Canada CEO John Clinton cited this example. When asked why Canadian banks were trusted by Canadians much more than banks in other nations were trusted by the citizens of those nations, he said:

> I think it's two things. Canadians believe they came through the banking crisis better than anybody else because of government regulation. I don't think they believe it's purely because of the banks. The second thing is equally important, and that is that you've had two unbelievable spokespeople for the banking system in Canada — Mark Carney and Jim Flaherty. Think about how consistent they have been about this story that we haven't got in trouble because we didn't do the stupid things that were done around the world. They've told that story in Iceland, the U.K. and the U.S. They've told it everywhere, and they've been very consistent about it.[xv]

SIZE DOES MATTER (SORT OF)

It's easy to assume that consistent communication is much easier in a smaller organization, but that would be untrue. At its core, consistency requires rigor and discipline, which can be at a greater risk of breaking down in smaller organizations. This can occur for several reasons, including the lack of in-house communications expertise that is typically a hallmark of smaller organizations. The structure and flow of information in small organizations are other factors that could compromise consistency.

Contrast this with the size of a global company with offices in many countries around the world. It employs hundreds of thousands of employees. How do you ensure employees in all those countries hear the same messages from their local "office" manager as they hear from their local country manager? Moving further up into the organization, how do you ensure that message remains consistent with the messages from a regional leader and then a set of global leaders?

The answer is that you ensure there is concrete planning and clear expectations of leaders when it comes to communication. That's how you ensure consistency. What do clear expectations look like in practice?

I have seen organizations ask leaders to cascade messages they receive from the most senior executive management. This is one important first step, ensuring that all employees receive the information from their manager or department or unit head. However, for some leaders the word "cascade" simply means "share" (e.g., present the content at a team meeting or forward it by email to team members). This is fundamentally different than explicitly asking others to ensure the messages conveyed are received as intended. To achieve this, one must do more than just "share" the messages. They have to be invested in ensuring employees understand them. This type of conversation can take place during existing team or departmental meetings, or if it's small team, by just checking in with employees. Some of the questions you should consider asking include: "You received the communication from our President on topic X. Did you understand it? Do you have any questions, comments, or concerns about it?" The is an effective "cascade." When advising leaders, you need to be prescriptive in spelling out what the expectations are and what a "cascade" looks like.

If this seems like a lot of effort, it's because it is. As I hope I've made clear, powerful, impactful leadership communication doesn't happen by chance. It's a deliberately orchestrated series of activities to ensure a consistent message is communicated. And knowing that communication involves both a sender and a receiver, it's critical to confirm with the receiver that they understood what was intended by the sender.

In fact, the value of this feedback from employees is immense since it will give you the insight needed to inform and shape future communications. Alison Davis, the CEO profiled at the start of this book, excelled at ensuring messages were heard and understood by her direct reports. She did this because she had experienced firsthand the benefits of committing to this consistently. Alison knew that only with employee feedback could she adjust the volume of "noise" around a particular topic, meaning increasing or decreasing the amount of focus on a message or topic to ensure everyone was on the same page. When would you want to increase "noise" about a topic?

Perhaps you have recently introduced a plan for a change in your organization. Let's assume that the feedback from the first announcement indicated that employees were either confused about what the planned change would mean for them or weren't supportive of the change. This type of insight would be invaluable as you planned both the content and timing of future communications, no?

In my roles over the years as head of corporate communications in organizations, I have established a routine practice of distributing the slides used on leadership calls to the participants. I have asked that they share these with their direct reports and have included notes in the PowerPoint file. Other times, I have developed and distributed a set of key messages on an important topic to help ensure there is consistency across the organization when it comes to employees being informed about a given topic.

BE A FEEDBACK FANATIC

We've already discussed the benefits of bringing employees into the conversation. But if you really want to maximize these benefits, then in addition to circling back to gain feedback, look at other channels. It's easy to assume that, because you (or someone from your communications team) develop a message that in your opinion is crystal clear, said message will be heard exactly as you intended. But we know that humans are more complex than that.

They consider what they hear in the context of everything else they hear and experience. Why take a chance when you can mitigate that risk by simply asking employees if they understood, agreed, or supported (or insert any verb here) what you have communicated?

I guarantee you will find becoming a feedback fanatic invaluable as it will provide you with insight on how your messages are resonating with employees. You will be able to quickly discern whether what you are saying is considered clear and credible. And by the way, doing so will reinforce your commitment to transparent communication and help strengthen connections. Some feedback tools you may find useful include:

- Integrating a comments feature on your company intranet
- Creating small, informal forums or roundtables for open discussions with employees
- Ensuring there is always time allocated for Q&A after team, departmental, or company town halls
- Establishing an "Ask Me Anything" column on the company intranet where employee questions and your responses are shared broadly.

KEY TAKEAWAYS

- Consistent communication requires planning, forethought, rigor, and discipline.
- As a leader, you need to explicitly link messages to one another to reinforce consistency.
- Consistency is highly interrelated with other leadership attributes and traits such as competence, character, and credibility; maintain it to avoid a damaging domino effect.
- Consistent communication must be reinforced with actions that support the words.
- Plan for communications after a key offsite meeting to ensure consistency.
- Only selectively use absolutes such as "always" and "never."
- Qualifying statements can help you avoid being boxed in by something you have said.
- Heightened sensitivity is required to maintain consistency when communicating under pressure.

KEEP ~~OUT~~ IN:
TRANSPARENCY LIVES HERE

"A lack of transparency results in distrust and a
deep sense of insecurity."

— *The Dalai Lama*

Employees know more than we often give them credit for. They can sense when things aren't right, when something they have been told differs from what they experience. And if they really are our most valuable asset, why do we fail to tell them the truth?

Transparent communication can be difficult because we tend to avoid talking about the truth when we believe it will upset others or ourselves. We recognize it can create anxiety and/or confusion, and a range of other emotions, so when it puts us or our organizations in an unfavourable light, we tend to steer clear. However, if you are the kind of leader who avoids communicating transparently, you're actually creating more problems than you're solving. Here's why.

When employees feel as though they aren't getting the truth, it fuels unproductive, unhealthy water cooler talk. In the absence of information, or what they believe is truthful information, employees are like anyone else: they inevitably fill the vacuum that a lack of transparency has left empty with assumptions and information that paint a picture usually more inaccurate — and more negative — than reality. When this happens, it forces leaders and organizations to spend valuable time, energy, and resources addressing the rumours.

In fact, I would bet more time is spent on addressing the fallout from such water cooler talk than it would take a leader to just be transparent from the outset.

Think of it this way: if in fact "a lack of transparency results in distrust and a deep sense of insecurity" as the Dalai Lama suggests, what kind of negative impact on behaviour could this feeling of insecurity create in the workplace? Science tells us that people respond to feelings of insecurity in many different ways. When people feel insecure, the "fight" response kicks in: insecurity is a subset of feeling threatened. Therefore, when employees feel threatened, it has the potential to unleash a series of unintended consequences, that, taken together, can wreak havoc. This is because employees like predictability as much as anyone else. Many don't perform well in the conditions that non-transparent communication creates: uncertainty and ambiguity.

At one end of the spectrum — and I have witnessed this in more than one organization — employees who feel insecure seek employment elsewhere. And as we have already established, involuntary departures can be costly for an organization.

Along the spectrum, we see a host of other possible outcomes from employees feeling insecure. For example, how do you believe insecure employees perform? Is their focus compromised? Do you think their productivity increases or decreases when they feel this way? What about the energy they contribute to the company culture? Do you think it's positive when they are feeling threatened or negative? Will they be motivated to go that lauded "extra mile" when their emotional state is marked by anxiety and uncertainty? I thought so.

DIVERSITY OF THOUGHT

If you consider transparency through a different lens, one that is focused on value-creation, the potential benefits of communicating transparently increase exponentially. Quite simply, the more your employees know and have context for decisions you've made, plans you will implement, and actions you're considering taking, the better prepared they are to understand and support you in achieving what you have shared.

Equally important is the fact that they can provide feedback, contribute ideas, and suggest solutions. Think of it this way: when you bring employees into the dialogue about a topic, you have suddenly and significantly expanded your pool of thinking. All of this can help to strengthen and refine your original thinking, which will lead to better outcomes. It also drives stronger connections with employees because they feel included in the decision-making or problem-solving process and therefore more valued.

Dan Price, CEO of Gravity Payments, a company focused on processing payments for small businesses, took the notion of diversity of thought to a whole new level during the COVID-19 pandemic in 2020. When faced with the difficult decision to lay off 20% of his employees or go bankrupt, he refused to accept either option. Instead, he asked his employees what to do. According to *Fast Company*'s Elizabeth Shegran, "Price called a companywide meeting to let employees know the state of the business, and 40 hour-long meetings with small groups of employees were scheduled to gather ideas." And what followed was a classic lesson in transparent communication and trust-building. "We just put all our cards on the table," Price says. "And we listened." In the end, they came up with an approach that allowed every employee to share privately what they could afford to give up in terms of compensation to help keep the company afloat. Pretty powerful result.

BUILD ALIGNMENT

Engaging employees with transparent communication has other benefits too. An article in the magazine *Inc.* summed it up this way: "When you tell the truth, employees are more likely to feel that everyone's playing on the same team."[xvi]

This feeling of camaraderie has a positive impact on the level of collaboration in any company. It creates a "halo effect" grounded in a sense of shared interests and goals. Once that happens, the conditions are ripe for building alignment, and better aligned organizations operate more efficiently and deliver stronger business performance.

But it's not enough for people to know they belong a team: they need to *feel* it. A sense of belonging isn't a fact, it's an experience. And when that experience is a positive one, like the kind that occurs when people feel part of something bigger than themselves, they will feel better about their work environment.

Now pause and ask yourself: When employees feel better about their work environment and have a positive work experience, do they tend to be more engaged? The answer is yes. And when employees are more engaged, organizations deliver better results.

EMPLOYEE ENGAGEMENT

Gallup, a global analytics and advice firm, has conducted an annual meta-analysis since 1997 focused on the relationship between engagement at work and organizational outcomes.

In 2016, it released its findings for the meta-analysis from that year including the examination of 82,000 business units, 1.8 million employees, in 49 industries across 73 countries. Results show that business units with top-quartile engagement results outperformed bottom-quartile units by 10%, with profitability 21% higher for top-quartile companies.[xvii]

But Gallup is not alone. Google "employee engagement and impact on an organization's performance" and you will get access to endless articles, studies, and websites that will validate what Gallup found. In fact, at the time of writing, typing these words into the venerable search engine yields more than 64,000,000 results. Yes, sixty-four *million*!

Most importantly, we know that leaders are a key driver of employee engagement with their effectiveness directly tied to an employee's experience at work. In an article on Forbes.com, researcher Joseph Folkman writes: "The evidence is clear that high levels of employee engagement drive improved customer satisfaction, which impacts bottom-line profits. The effectiveness of an individual leader is a key factor influencing engagement and this also impacts retention of talented employees, discretionary effort in the organization and organizational profitability."[xviii]

Given the link between engagement and business performance, it's no surprise that culture and engagement are seen as the most important issue companies face around the world. Eighty-seven percent of organizations cite culture and engagement as one of their top challenges, while 50 percent call the problem "very important," according to global consultancy Deloitte.[xix]

How much can communication and the way a leader connects with their employees impact an organization's culture? In short, a lot. But it takes work.

NO ONE SAID IT WAS EASY

Without a doubt, there are challenges in creating a culture of transparency. One such challenge is the type of information that is communicated by leaders. Many times, leaders (and their communications teams) spend considerable time communicating *what* is going on in their organizations. That is, they focus on particular decisions and actions rather than on providing a broader narrative to explain those decisions that is rich in context.

Context is critical and often glossed over in preparing and delivering communications. Too much emphasis is placed on the messaging as opposed to spending time on explaining the content of the message itself. This has become especially widespread over the past five years as the growth of social media and "soundbite news" has expanded exponentially. In short, people tend to keep communications too brief.

Leaders must remember that employees are the same as everyone else and need to make sense of the information they receive. Often leaders are focused on the "what" (the expected result or outcome) of a decision. Or, they stay at a level too broad and general when communicating the "why" of a decision or action rather than sharing in simple, plain language the rationale for a decision — the context. Worse, they also frequently rely on corporate jargon that only confuses an otherwise simple message.

In fact, corporate jargon has become such a problem in communications that annual top ten lists and parodies abound making fun of the worst offenders. When communicating, it's critical you remember that employees were not part of all the discussion, debate, and/or analysis that took place behind closed doors that helped formulate a decision or approach.

As a leader, it's your responsibility to spend time bringing employees up to speed to the point where you've already arrived in your thinking. You can't assume that employees will understand what "leveraging cross-functional synergies," "optimizing manufacturing to create efficiencies," or "decentralizing and streamlining the organizational structure" means. When language like this is used, the actual meaning of your message can easily get "lost in translation."

By staying too high-level or using too much corporate jargon and not explaining the thought process and alternatives that were considered, the leader is essentially saying "just trust us, we've got this covered." The challenge with that assumption, as Jeff Ansell says, "Trust is not something you can simply tell people to have. Trust is something that must be earned."[xx] Transparent communication is one important way to earn that trust.

If you are going to use corporate jargon — and let's face it, there is an economy of words that is created when it is used — also include an explanation: "What I mean by ... is this." This enables you to provide the context and meaning behind the words.

At times, I've worked with leaders who shy away from transparency because they know that certain information will generate dissenting points of view. They are either non-confrontational by nature and would rather not invite a potentially difficult conversation, or perhaps are too self-absorbed, thinking they alone have all the right answers. None of these provide a productive approach.

Truth be told, if you're looking to build trust, there is no better way than asking your stakeholders to be part of the dialogue. Foster an environment where employees are free to speak their mind. Then you'll at least know what they're thinking and where they stand on a matter. Take the guesswork out of the equation. If you are concerned that your perspective will be different than theirs, or you don't want to be caught off-guard by having to respond in the moment, try using a transition statement which can help to diffuse defensiveness or unproductive, tension-filled discourse.

One such transition I really like comes from Jim Gray, author of *How Leaders Speak*. His respectful but firm transition is simply, "I see things differently." [xxi] In this manner, you are not discounting another's view or opinion, just simply communicating that you don't share that opinion. You can strengthen this response even further by acknowledging the other person's position. Something like, "I can see that you feel very strongly about this and I respect that. I see things (a little) differently."

Notice the absence of the words "however" or "but" in the second response. These words can undermine or negate someone's point of view, and only reinforces you coming across as either rigid in your perspective or a know-it-all — maybe even both.

These are small, specific steps, but all ladder up to making sure people feel heard and will go a long way toward building connections and trust. Again, no one said this was easy!

WHERE LEADERSHIP AND COMMUNICATION OVERLAP

For people like me who advise leaders on matters of communication and reputation management (personal and organizational), it's important to have a strong and clear understanding of what gets in the way of transparency. It's also obviously important for someone to have their own understanding of this issue as well. As you reflect on this aspect of your leadership development, ask yourself: What's at the root of my behaviour when I feel like I can't be transparent? Who benefits when I act this way? Honest self-awareness is essential before you can realistically change your behaviour.

Understanding your leadership style also provides clues to your communication style. The two are closely linked. For example, one leader I worked with — I will call him Ted — was the kind of person who preferred a micro-management approach. Ted wanted to be involved in every decision, large or small, instead of empowering other leaders to, well, lead! This leadership style also shaped his approach to communications.

Not only did this mean that Ted wanted to see, approve, and often modify all content that was shared with employees, it also meant he decided to hold back much of the information that would have been valuable for employees to know (the context). This included the rationale for significant decisions that were made by the management team and financial information that would have been valuable for other leaders to know so they could make informed decisions about how to best operate the company.

To this day, I'm still at a loss as to why Ted took this approach, since I saw firsthand the negative impact that it had on others and the organization more broadly. So I have rationalized it this way: either he didn't believe his own words, or he couldn't handle potential criticism of his thinking. Either way, this approach did not help build trust.

This approach also negatively impacted transparency among Ted's direct reports. This meant that before every management team meeting all information to be discussed or presented was shared with him ahead of time. This fuelled an avoidance of any productive debate (a.k.a. disagreement) during meetings, which negatively impacted the level of engagement among the executives.

Recall what Jack Welch said about hoarding information. Sharing financial information is an incredibly valuable way to help employees understand what they need to do more or less of to drive better performance. They need the context of financials. This doesn't mean that you need to share every detail or potentially highly sensitive information (e.g., gross margin, operating income, EBITDA, COGS, etc.), but enough information that will provide direction to your teams and enable them to make informed decisions. It helps build empowerment and alignment, which, as we know, drives employee engagement.

From a broader employee perspective, understanding how their organization is performing financially can be quite motivating (if the company is performing well that is!). If it isn't meeting its targets, sharing the information anyway poses a unique opportunity to showcase how leadership will address any gaps, which can build confidence in leadership and serve as an inspiration for some employees.

In some situations, you can demonstrate the highest level of transparency by engaging employees in finding solutions to the challenges, to take an even more active role in the performance of the company. This could include them making an increased effort to sustain performance momentum, or helping their organization get back on track if performance is lagging.

In one organization I worked with, once management started sharing financial information, the number one comment received in every single employee survey was how appreciative employees were for the open and transparent manner of communication. It also served as a powerful enabler of financial discipline in the company, which only increased as employees had more access to the numbers. Quite simply, information is (em)power(ing): don't hold it back.

TRANSPARENCY WITH CONSTRAINTS

Transparent communication is effective for many reasons, but its importance is underscored most when there are constraints. One common scenario of constraints occurs when difficult, performance-related conversations take place between a manager (a.k.a. a "leader") and one of their direct reports. Often, the road more travelled is to avoid these conversations altogether.

This was clearly the case in Justin's scenario, as he was on his third performance review at his company before he learned he was no longer on the CEO track. Was his manager's avoidance of the transparent discussion with Justin really setting Justin up for success? Of course not. But clearly his manager forgot a fundamental rule of leadership: it's not about you!

For many, ignoring difficult conversations is simply easier than the potential tension, hurt feelings, denial, and anger that can emerge as an outcome. However, avoidance inevitably leads to a range of significant other problems. These include the negative impact on the rest of the team's morale and engagement when they don't see underperformance managed effectively. I have witnessed this many times in my own career, and have seen firsthand the repercussions: employee attrition, lost productivity and loss of respect and trust for the leader. Any of these outcomes costs an organization money as well as a negative impact on performance.

If you don't believe that non-transparent communication could actually cost your organization money, think again. We know from research shared earlier in this chapter that transparent communication is linked to employee engagement. We also know that employee engagement is linked to the performance of an organization. Therefore, if engagement suffers, there is a risk that performance will as well. Why take that risk?

Here is a personal anecdote of where my lack of transparent communication almost cost the company I was working for some business. It occurred almost 20 years ago when I was working for a

PR agency. I had been appointed to lead one of the larger and more valuable accounts at the agency and was assigned a small team to help manage the account. Though I had suspected that the account I was managing was in trouble, based on some emails I had been copied in on as well as some subtle comments from the team, I did not approach the team directly with my concerns. I was a very young executive, not much older than the team I managed, and I wanted to connect with them more as their friend than as their superior.

By the time I pushed for a status review of how the assignment was progressing, it had fallen almost entirely off the rails, marked by missed deadlines and budget overruns. Transparent conversations about performance were just not taking place, and it was my responsibility to initiate them. Fortunately, the account was eventually saved and remained with the firm, but it could have just as easily gone the other way.

The truth is that managing underperformance not only takes courage, but also time. A 2018 survey by global staffing firm Robert Half asked CFOs to estimate how much time is spent coaching underperforming employees. The answer: 26% of working hours, on average — that's over ten hours out of a forty-hour workweek. Finance executives also acknowledged that hiring mistakes negatively affected team morale.[xxii] This provides further evidence of the value-eroding impact created by not communicating transparently with underperformers.

Ironically, another more obvious scenario where transparent communication is frequently tested is during crises. Yet these are precisely the times when people demand and need to know the truth. It provides them reassurance and comfort to know that they are being communicated with in a straight-up manner. Typically, there is a reluctance on the part of leaders and organizations to share everything they know during a crisis, and the reasons for this vary.

One reason is that leaders often believe they must have all the information first before sharing anything. The reality, though, is that the natural evolution of most crises means that one must operate (e.g., make decisions, communicate with stakeholders) in the absence of perfect information. Remember the qualifying statements covered in the previous chapter on consistency, as these can be valuable in enabling you to communicate honestly, with integrity, and transparently:

- "Here is what I/we know at this point in time…"
- "What I can share with you today is…"
- "I won't say never … but what I can tell you is…"

A second reason leaders are reluctant to communicate transparently during crises is the *fear of commitment*. This means they fear being tied to their comments in a situation that is rapidly evolving. I understand this completely, but the vast majority of people will cut you some slack if they know you are being transparent with them in the first place. And again, the qualifying statements can be a useful tool here to help mitigate the impact of verbal comments or commitments not upheld.

Lastly, and this is probably the most challenging barrier to overcome for leaders interested in communicating transparently during crises, is the concern that sharing "too much" information will add to the heightened anxiety that is a hallmark of crises. My experience from leading communications during several crises, however, is that the unvarnished truth often allays people's concerns because they have at least some information to help them cope and make sense of the crisis. This is the exact situation played out earlier in this book that highlighted what happens when there is a vacuum of information: people tend to fill that vacuum with information that is far more inaccurate than reality. For example, employees hear that two of the most senior leaders have left the company unexpectedly but there is no "formal" communication about their exit. Immediately, those who either worked directly with the leaders or even know them begin to posit ideas for why they left in the absence of being provided this information. In doing so, they ascribe their own ideas or beliefs about what happened, based on their own personal experience of these leaders or what they might have heard their colleagues experience with these leaders. The fact is though, that employees' beliefs and ideas aren't, well ... facts. There are both practical and other reasons why it isn't always possible or appropriate to announce the exit of a leader. I understand that. However, as discussed throughout this book, it's about being deliberate in making that decision versus defaulting to an established or familiar process. Yet time and again there are concrete examples of leaders failing to leverage this principle of the Trust Trifecta to their benefit and the benefit of those they serve.

Let's return to the COVID-19 outbreak and consider President Trump's communication strategy. From his refusal to comply with key transparency measures in his coronavirus stimulus bill,[xxiii] to NPR's coverage of demands by lawmakers for more transparency from the administration about their coronavirus response, critics came out from all corners to weigh in on the issue of transparency.[xxiv] In short, President Trump received poor grades on the transparency of his communication.

IT TAKES TWO TO TANGO ... AND TALK!

Dialogue is a two-way street. Remember that powerful and effective communication is not just transmission of information. To truly embed a transparent communications approach, think about all the channels your organization uses to communicate with its stakeholders.

For example, does your company intranet have a feature that allows employees to comment on posted content? Have you turned on the comments section for your Twitter handle or corporate LinkedIn page? Each of the platforms and channels you use represents a powerful opportunity to create firsthand, unfiltered dialogue directly with your organization's stakeholders.

The political arena is one space where we see dialogue being strategically employed. Nowadays, even before campaigns officially begin, the latest trend is for candidates to host "town halls."

Even major news networks such as CNN have jumped on this bandwagon by regularly hosting and televising their own town halls. This gives political candidates an opportunity to hear directly from the stakeholders they are trying to win over. It's also a chance for them to display their own transparency, which for political leaders is frequently a larger struggle than it is for their private and non-profit sector counterparts.

The need for transparency (or at a minimum, perceived transparency) is well understood by politicians. They appreciate the fact that a large segment of the electorate is cynical about politics and politicians. Perhaps that's why in 2007, then-senator Barack Obama pledged he would lead the "most transparent and accountable administration in history."[xxv] This was followed less than a year later by opponent Senator John McCain saying in May 2008, "My administration will set a new standard for transparency and accountability."[xxvi]

In many ways, both of these politicians kept their word by releasing detailed personal health and financial records along with other documents (note the role of consistency here, words being supported by actions). Moreover, both McCain and Obama's declarations were in stark contrast with presidential candidates from the 2016 election, termed "the no-transparency election" by CNN.[xxvii]

Interestingly, despite low transparency (not to mention his inconsistent communication, lack of political experience and questionable character), Trump won the contest in part because of how he gained voters' trust. More on that later.

TRANSPARENCY IN TRANSFORMATIONS

One sign of the positive impact transparent communication can have inside organizations shows up when you consider companies experiencing significant or transformational change. In these cases, I have heard it assumed that employee engagement can be expected to take a hit because of the uncertainty and anxiety that profound organizational change can foster.

However, I've been part of two multinational organizations that experienced significant, multi-year transformations where employee engagement scores either remained the same (give or take a percentage point or two) or even increased. When I reviewed the broader analytics to find out what else could contribute to these results, I was unsurprised to find that the sentiment of transparent communication and strong leadership were both clearly represented.

In one of the companies, almost every single exit interview of employees who were impacted by the transformation said they appreciated the transparency of communication over the preceding eighteen months. It allowed them to know exactly what was happening and when, which they found to be empowering as they prepared for a possible life and career after exiting the organization.

Similar to other forms of communication, the impact of transparent communication during restructurings is also supported by published studies. In their paper titled, "The impact of positivity and transparency on trust in leaders and their perceived effectiveness," Steven M. Norman, Bruce J. Avolio, and Fred Luthans found both the leader's level of positivity and transparency impacted followers' perceived trust and evaluations of leader effectiveness.[xxviii]

Thus, while being transparent can demand a lot from you as the leader — honesty, vulnerability, discomfort, and more — the benefits gained, especially for the people on the receiving end of your words, far outweigh the demands on you.

Yet despite all of the benefits of transparent communication, it remains in short supply these days.

Christine Lagarde, upon being nominated as the President of the European Central Bank in September 2019, highlighted this when she felt it necessary to state: "Don't overinterpret, don't second-guess, cross-reference. I'm going to be myself and therefore probably different. In other words: 'you take what I say at face value – I mean what I say.'"[xxix]

If you always keep the sentiment that "it's not about you" front and centre, then communicating transparently will become much, much easier. I promise.

KEY TAKEAWAYS

- A lack of transparency can be distracting and disruptive, fueling unproductive water cooler talk and derailing the messages a company wants to communicate.
- The use of corporate jargon can unintentionally negatively impact transparency because context and meaning can get lost, leaving employees and other stakeholders wondering if they were told the whole story.
- Transparency positively impacts employee morale, engagement, and retention, as well as individual and organizational performance.
- Being transparent draws employees in and can generate valuable insight and input that can be used to further advance an organization's goals.
- Transparent communication is easily compromised when constraints are present, (managing under-performance, transformations etc.) and an elevated focus is needed.
- Two-way dialogue epitomizes transparent communication and should be strongly encouraged with all of your stakeholders.

ALL HAIL AUTHENTICITY

*"Be human and be authentic. That's what people
need today more than anything else."*
— *Chuck Robbins, CEO, Cisco*

According to an article on insights.com about authentic leadership, most of us have two sides to our personality: the "work self" and the "non-work self." This leads us to behave in different ways from how we interact with others, to how we communicate with others. At work, we typically try to show the "professional" side of ourselves. Although I'm not exactly sure what that means, and I'm certain that it differs from person to person, what I have seen with people I have worked closely with, is a more formal approach. They change their behaviour and style to what they believe or perceive is necessary. It's as if they are more concerned with how others are viewing them, than just being "themselves." I agree there *are times* when formality is warranted. That's not even a debatable issue. But in the end, what is warranted *every time* is bringing your whole, natural, authentic self to work. Being "professional" and being "yourself" aren't mutually exclusive. As Chuck Robbins reflects in his quote above, "that's what people need today more than anything else."

Can you relate to this? Being authentic is the single area where I have seen leaders struggle the most. In addition to the factors highlighted above which often drive this struggle, I would add this: there is a particular way that leaders assume they ought to behave. Because of this, there is a deeply entrenched reluctance to let their guard down and just be who they naturally are while in the workplace.

Now don't get me wrong, I'm not suggesting you should speak at work exactly the way you do in your private life (not that employees would be shocked to learn that you also swear). Nor am I suggesting that you be an open book and bare your soul to your peers and direct reports. You have to make careful judgments about sharing certain types of information with employees or other stakeholders with whom you may interact. However, I *am* suggesting that you convey the same kind of compassion, sincerity, and honesty when you speak in a professional setting as you would during a conversation with one of your closest friends. This is the basis for making connections with others.

AUTHENTICITY IN A CRISIS

The challenge of authenticity is especially acute when difficult news must be delivered, whether it's company crises, dismissals, mergers, or any emotionally charged situation. Yet these are the exact times when employees (and other stakeholders) are hungering for that "human touch" (not literally!) that says, "I understand what you must be feeling" (shock, disappointment, anger, confusion, hurt, etc.) or "I sincerely apologize for…" They don't want to hear corporate messages, or worse, for those messages to be buried in corporate jargon.

At these times, more than any other, affected stakeholders just want you to demonstrate that you understand their experience. Though these expectations aren't explicitly stated, they are without mystery and, in fact, are the same that you would have in similar circumstances. Employees want the truth, and they want it shared in a meaningful way. It's called being human.

Just as in other aspects of communication, "crisis communication" is layered with many complexities, considerations and factors that can impact its authenticity.

Time pressure is one of these considerations because the two most important aspects of successful crisis communications are to be proactive and responsive. This means you typically don't have the luxury of time you normally do to develop the *ideal* key message(s). It's rare that all pertinent information is known in detail when that first communication is due to be delivered. Crises are times when the intersection between leadership and communication is highlighted in a profound way. They are the times when core leadership attributes, such as acting decisively in the face of ambiguity or in the absence of perfect information, must be demonstrated.

Legal counsel is another factor that may impact an authentic response in a crisis. Usually borne out of the need to protect an individual or organization from potential liability, the legal lens can frequently create a sentiment or message that lacks the required compassion, empathy, and honesty that stakeholders (and the public) are expecting to hear.

I have seen this play out many times during high profile, highly sensitive moments. As a leader, your role must be to ensure the appropriate balance between legal "cover," and the tone and content that is reasonably expected by everyone concerned. This is one of those tricky times when you will likely need to balance competing perspectives from multiple leaders in your organization.

Other factors also contribute to the mishandling of authentic communication during a crisis or challenging times. For some leaders, there is a mismatch between the severity of the situation and their associated communications: the communications come across as simply insufficient.

Other leaders have a naïve or misguided belief in their own invincibility, that somehow they, or their organizations, will be protected from having to answer for misdeeds. As a result, they can come across as arrogant. Regardless, it is easy to see how the words, channel, tone, and framing used to communicate during a crisis can dramatically affect a message and can either strengthen or erode trust in a leader or organization.

To highlight this, one needs only to take a stroll by the heap of wrecked corporate reputations to see it littered with examples illustrating how not to communicate during a crisis.

Unilever

In October 2017, the Dove brand issued the following Tweet after posting an ad on Facebook that was widely seen as discriminatory.

"An image we recently posted on Facebook missed the mark in representing women of colour thoughtfully. We deeply regret the offense it caused."[xxx]

To me, this is a predictable, formulaic and highly unsatisfying response primarily driven by six words: "missed the mark" and "regret the offense." The phrase "missed the mark" significantly diminishes the impact of the ad (i.e., how it might have made black women feel) and just appears dismissive.

It comes across that the ad and its fallout didn't seem like a significant issue for Unilever. If the company truly understood the experience this ad had created (as demonstrated by the flood of emotionally charged comments on social media), the company would have matched its response to this experience.

"Regret the offense" is similarly understated compared to what it should have been. It's the kind of phrase you might use when you should have invited some friends to dinner but excluded them. "I regret not inviting the Smiths, I didn't mean to offend them." What could Unilever have said? There are many different possibilities, but here is one:

> We showed an extraordinary lack of judgment in our recent ad that hurt many people. There is no excuse for it, and nothing we can say will erase the pain it caused. All we can do is offer our sincere apologies and promise to learn from this mistake.

If the company had decided to include this last part in their response (the promise to learn), they would have needed to spell out exactly what that would look like. Again, this is the consistency component of the Trust Trifecta, where behaviours or actions must support words.

United Airlines

On April 9, 2017, the world was shocked when a video of law enforcement officers forcibly dragging a passenger off a United Airlines flight went viral. The passenger, later identified as a 69-year-old Vietnamese-American doctor named David Dao, had refused to give up his seat when Flight 3411 was overbooked.

Astonishingly, the company's first response made no mention of the victim, Dr. Dao. "We apologize for the overbook situation" read, in part, the company's statement. Later, the company would clarify that the flight was not actually overbooked. As the video continued to spread on social media, the crisis reached a fever pitch.[xxxi]

In further response, United Airlines CEO Oscar Munoz released this statement:

> This is an upsetting event to all of us here at United. I apologize for having to re-accommodate these customers. Our team is moving with a sense of urgency to work with the authorities and conduct our own detailed review of what happened. We are also reaching out to this passenger to talk directly to him and further address and resolve this situation.[xxxii]

Even with their second opportunity, United missed the mark. How? Their response spoke only to the operational aspects of their business — "re-accommodate these customers" — and lacked total empathy for the victim. I'm not sure what they were hoping to gain from "reaching out to this passenger to talk directly to him and further address and resolve this situation," because it seems like the situation was resolved, just not in a manner that, to most people, seemed remotely acceptable.

How could United have handled it differently? Most importantly, they needed to understand all of the stakeholders who were impacted by this incident. Only by identifying them in a discrete way (United Airlines employees, the other passengers, David Dao himself) could they have been in a position to consider prioritizing communications for each stakeholder, and then customizing the messages for each stakeholder.

Clearly, to any observer, the most important stakeholder in this situation was Dr. Dao. Therefore, while it was important to be sensitive and speak to the other passengers that were impacted by this event, I wouldn't have addressed the problem of passenger inconvenience (e.g., by re-accommodating them on another flight) in the company's first statement. Doing so just distracted from the core purpose of what the statement should have been focused on, which was an apology to David Dao. I would have spoken to the fact that this situation created a highly upsetting and emotional experience for all of the people who had no choice but to witness it. But the truly egregious oversight in this statement is an apology that should have been directly aimed at Dr. Dao.

In beginning their apology by sharing how upsetting the event was for the airline's employees, I can't imagine what the company was hoping for in terms of a response from Dr. Dao, let alone the broader court of public opinion. How is that supposed to make the reader of said apology feel? Was United asking us to feel bad that their employees felt bad? What about feeling bad for Dr. Dao, the actual victim?

Southwest Airlines

Months after the more famous United Airlines incident, Southwest Airlines called the police on a passenger who said she was allergic to another passenger's service animal; chaos ensued.

"We are disheartened by the way this situation unfolded and the customer's removal by local law enforcement officers," [xxxiii] the company said.

Terms like "disheartened" feel disingenuous. To me, disheartened says you "felt bad." They could have picked any number of other more emotive and powerful words to describe what they really "felt" or ought to have "felt." Some that come to mind include ashamed, embarrassed, shocked, deeply concerned; anything other than "disheartened." Words matter.

Moreover, if you watch the video and see how the customer was dragged down the aisle of the plane, using the word "disheartened" just feels far too inadequate to describe the incident.

The fact is, passenger security must absolutely be the focus of all airlines. Most reasonable people inherently understand this. I can appreciate that the situation may not have resolved itself without officers removing a passenger who was being disorderly. But unless you were one of the passengers on that plane and saw firsthand all the steps the airline and police took to resolve the situation before it escalated to physical removal, you might find it very difficult to take the airline's side in this situation. This is a place where context is essential.

"A traumatic situation unfolded on one of our flights today that was unavoidable." This is how an apology could have begun. It immediately provides a clear picture of what happened. It was something traumatic (for not just the impacted passenger, but for others who experienced it up close). Using the word "unavoidable" also instantly conveys that the final action taken by the airline was a measure of last resort.

The apology could have followed the initial statement, with additional information, to further make clear the context for what occurred:

> After multiple requests to the disorderly passenger to resolve the situation off the plane, we were unfortunately forced to physically remove her for the safety of the other passengers. We could not risk this situation being further escalated and becoming outside of our control. We appreciate this was extremely upsetting for both the affected passenger and all those who witnessed her removal, and for that we apologize sincerely.

Volkswagen

After the scandal over revelations that the auto giant had developed software that allowed it to cheat on the emissions standards tests for its diesel vehicles, Volkswagen's US head Michael Horn appeared on Capitol Hill to explain the company's position to federal lawmakers.

Although Horn offered a "sincere apology for Volkswagen's use of a software program that served to defeat the emissions testing program," he also was quick to explain it away.

"This was a couple of software engineers who put this in for whatever reason," Horn said to the House of Representatives Oversight and Investigations Committee, according to NBC News. "This was not a corporate decision. There was no board meeting that approved this."[xxxiv]

Unfortunately, absolving oneself from the issue, or in this case, absolving an entire company, only weakens a "sincere apology." Accountability from leadership during times of crisis is imperative, and any approach that detracts from this will only diminish or eliminate an authentic message.

Each of these cases, like countless other examples from the political arena, the sports world, and the entertainment sector, showcase the struggle leaders seem to have being authentic and transparent when things go wrong. They illuminate what Eric Dezenhall calls the "glass jaw" (in his book of the same name) — "the idea the powerful are brittle under certain conditions."[xxxv] This is important to recognize, because there can be an element of perceived invincibility when a crisis occurs. It is borne out of arrogance, ignorance, or just simple naïveté.

Dezenhall also shares the insight that while authenticity is paramount during crises, and leaders and organizations are "hard marked" (i.e., judged more harshly) for how they respond, authenticity goes beyond a one-off event.

This is another powerful reminder of the consistency principle from the Trust Trifecta. All actions and behaviours by an organization or its leaders must be sustained on an ongoing basis. The first time for displaying authenticity and the principles of the Trust Trifecta should not be during a crisis. If a leader or organization is interested in protecting or strengthening their corporate reputation, they should always remember that people trust those they believe. And they believe those that behave and communicate in a consistent way as part of their regular course of business.

SPOTLIGHT ON STARBUCKS

As these few examples show, there are clearly times when leaders drop the ball and fumble in their communications, especially during crises. However, there are an equal number of touchdowns as well.

Consider Starbucks. In April 2018, the prominent global brand faced a significant reputational threat when an employee called the police because two black men would not order any food or drinks. The two men had told the Starbuck's employee they were just there for a meeting, but soon left in handcuffs after the police arrived. The employee's actions set off a firestorm marked by protesters in front of the store calling for boycotts and the label "racist" being attached to the coffee chain.

CEO Kevin Johnson responded immediately, substantively, and, most importantly, consistently. In an interview with CNN, Johnson said he personally was accountable for the actions of the employee (note how different his position was from that of Horn's on employees acting without support from the Board). Johnson also said that it signalled that something had to be done within the culture of Starbucks. "This is one step. This is not the only step," he said when referring to reaching an agreement with the two men at the centre of the controversy.[xxxvi] For Johnson, this wasn't just an "incident" but a wake-up call to something larger that was going on at Starbucks, and readily admitting that is the epitome of transparency.

But he didn't stop there. He didn't just apologize in a sincere manner. Kevin supported his words with the following actions:

- He began to personally mentor the two men (who were entrepreneurs).
- He closed 8,000 locations for one day and provided anti-bias training to 175,000 employees.
- He had 12 additional modules on diversity developed and deployed over time to Starbucks employees.

WHERE'S THE PROOF?

I've been asked before, and indeed challenged on, whether or not there is a concrete benefit to managing crises effectively. Yes, is my answer. Though perhaps not easily measurable, a well-managed crisis is one part of effective reputation management. Translated into concrete terms, a well-managed crisis means support for a brand and support for a leader. Conversely, a poorly managed crisis can mean the loss of existing or future customers. It's very difficult to be precise in these cases with respect to a financial impact, but it is well documented that a company's reputation is a deciding factor in purchasing decisions.

But there are examples where a poorly managed crisis can result in a material financial impact.

Consider Facebook. According to one report from CNBC, "Facebook shares fell almost 5 percent on March 27 when reports broke that Zuckerberg had decided to testify before Congress. The decision came as pressure mounted on Facebook, following the Cambridge Analytica scandal. Just one day prior, the Federal Trade Commission announced that it would investigate Facebook's data practices. The day cost Facebook's market cap nearly $23 billion."[xxxvii]

AUTHENTICITY ALWAYS

While it's clear that authenticity is especially critical during crises, it will help any leader to have this as their default communications stance. That is, incorporate authenticity consistently in communications. One such example of a leader who I have seen use this approach is Alex Gorsky, CEO of Johnson & Johnson.

On November 9, 2016, he sent an internal memo to employees that fulfilled all criteria of the Trust Trifecta. It began with this context setting and transparent set up:

> The presidential campaign in the United States is finally over, and the result stunned the experts and political establishment in America and around the world. Now that the confetti has fallen and the last political ads have finally flickered and faded from view, it is time to ask the one really important question: Now what?

By asking this question from the outset, Gorsky was acknowledging in a very transparent way that J&J employees were likely wondering what it meant for the 130-year-old company. So he answered his own question to remove any doubt about where he expected the company to stand:

> When the campaign promises, accusations and claims are long forgotten, the United States goes on as a nation, as a people. The world goes on. The president-elect has called for us to build the future together, to heal the bitter divisions. That is most important now.

He knew that the 130,000 employees at J&J comprised people of a variety of political stripes, but he used the opportunity in a very authentic way to set expectations for moving forward. "An inscription on the national seal of the United States tells us how to do that: E Pluribus Unum. That Latin phrase translates to: 'from many, one.' From different people of different backgrounds, from many different interests and many opinions, from many talents, strengths and aspirations we are one nation. Now we go forward together. We meet our challenges and opportunities together."

The entire communication was written in a way that was so consistent with all of Alex's other communications, even though this specific topic was rife with opportunities to make a misstep. And, as if to ensure nothing was left to chance in the minds of employees, Mr. Gorsky was especially clear about the way forward for J&J during Donald Trump's administration.

> As a company, of course, Johnson & Johnson does not take sides in presidential elections. And our employees represent virtually every political viewpoint. But in the U.S., whether red or blue in politics before the election, now we are all red, white and blue. Together, we will stand by the side of our new president, just as we have done with the current and past administrations. And, we will continue to support the Congress and all state and local leaders. Our future and the future of our children and grandchildren depend on that.[xxxviii]

Leaders often struggle with saying what they mean and "putting themselves out there." Gorsky did not.

Pride and self-preservation all work against leaders in high stakes, high pressure situations. Recognizing, accepting, and actively managing these is a critical part of effective, authentic communication.

But as with all communication, authentic communication is more an art than a science. And authenticity may not always be appropriate in every setting.

Jeff Ansell highlighted this with the case of publishing mogul Conrad Black: "On trial for tax fraud and obstructing justice, Black, who owned four luxurious homes and two dozen cars asserted that a typical Chicago jury member who 'does not reside in more than one residence, employ servants or a chauffeur, enjoy lavish furniture, or host expensive parties' should not be considered one of his peers."[xxxix]

Black was being his authentic self and should get points for that, yet I am reluctant to award them to him!

CAN AUTHENTICITY BE LEARNED?

Bill George, the creator of "authentic leadership" and Senior Fellow at Harvard Business School, stated in a July 2016 article that the "debate over which form of leadership works best seems settled, in my view. Most leading companies globally are focusing on developing 'authentic leaders' within their ranks."[xl] Executive courses at Harvard Business School in authentic leadership development are oversubscribed and expanding every year. As the *Harvard Business Review* declared in January 2015, "Authenticity has emerged as the gold standard for leadership."[xli]

This reality — that Harvard teaches courses on authentic leadership — flies in the face of the assumption that authenticity can't be learned. But with honest self-reflection, self-awareness, and feedback from others, any leader can get an insightful view of how they are "showing up" when interacting with others. The caution to anyone seeking this path is to accept that it's not merely an intellectual exercise. You need to put real, honest work into changing how you communicate and connect with others. In other words, you need to be more like Alison than Justin.

Many leaders I have worked with over the years have been told how they come across to others and yet they haven't changed. These are intelligent, capable people who have the capacity to understand and apply the learnings from this feedback, but they don't.

My position on these leaders is that it arises because of an unwillingness to set aside ego and perceived expectations about how they ought to behave. It all gets back to the "V" word: vulnerability. When leaders become willing to be exposed to emotional harm or injury, only then will they truly be able to reveal their authentic selves. Justin Ray, the know-it-all, accomplish-it-all superstar, is one such example of not applying feedback.

Authenticity is powered by deep conviction and transparency. It means being willing to share information that you are not comfortable sharing. In fact, if you let your discomfort show, even better. Just be yourself and let the words flow.

If we refer back to the 2016 election, this point is illuminated further. Clinton was articulate, insightful and provided countless concrete examples to substantiate the points she was making. She was credible. None of this made a difference because she didn't come across as "warm." She didn't connect with people, and as a result, people felt as though they didn't know her. Of the many headlines that dotted the media landscape after the election, this one from the BBC's website summed it up quite succinctly: "Who is the Real Hillary Clinton?" In the article, the BBC captured the essence of Hillary's fundamental challenge in its first paragraph: "For someone who has faced such scrutiny, few people feel they know the 'real' Hillary Clinton. Many Americans just don't trust her."[xlii]

Contrast that with the Hillary who sat down with Howard Stern for a two-plus hour chat in December 2019. She laughed. She joked. She shared. Pundits had a field day with the interview with more than one asking, if she had behaved this way in the 2008 or 2016 election, would it have made a difference? This isn't to simplify things by suggesting that if Clinton went on air with Stern in either of those elections it would have been the difference maker. However, the truth likely lies somewhere in the middle. That is, if Hillary acted more like herself during those elections, perhaps more people would have warmed up to her. After all, those who know her well confirmed that the way she carried herself with Stern in December 2019 is the "real Hillary."

The takeaway? *You have to feel like you know someone in order to trust them.*

"Feel" is the operative word here. It's not only about facts and stats. Americans for the most part either knew about Hillary's track record or ought to have known. But we are emotional by nature as humans, and what we feel, that intangible essence, can be difficult to tap into.

In short, Hillary would have scored high on competence, but low on trust and the principles of the Trust Trifecta.

Contrast that with Trump, who according to the *Guardian* was "wildly ill-disciplined. There was outrageous behaviour and offensive statements that alienated women, African Americans, Mexicans, Muslims, disabled people and, ultimately, believers in constitutional democracy."[xliii]

Yet there is something undeniable about how he connected (and continues to connect) with millions of people. At its core, the secret is that he is always his "true self." Trump reeked of authenticity in that it was clear that he genuinely believed what he was saying at the moment he said it. His no-filter approach to communicating was also transparent. He just said what he really thought and didn't care who might be caught in the crosshairs or what the ramifications might be from his reckless use of words.

To be clear, my only point here is about how Trump connected with voters through his style of communication. I am not endorsing what he said back then or the way he communicates today. Nor am I suggesting that his behaviour back then and since then is remotely appropriate or that I support his treatment of others or his policy positions. Lastly, I'm not suggesting his use of social media channels to share his messages is the best approach. However, it's hard to disagree that he connected with his base primarily because of the way he communicated.

Among those outside his base, he would have likely scored low on competence, character, and credibility, but what about when it comes to the Trust Trifecta? Let's consider consistency. Here Trump only gets part marks, because while he was consistent in communicating his key message — "Make America Great Again" — he loses marks for the multiple occasions when he flip-flopped on his policy views or positions that he had taken. Transparency? Another assumed driver of trust where he would have likely scored low due to the clear and compelling evidence that he hasn't always shared the "full story."

That leaves authenticity, the highest valued driver of trust. Chip and Dan Heath in their book *Made to Stick* write, "What matters to people? People matter to themselves."[xliv] Trump understood this and tapped into the self-interest of many voters when he spoke to them. His communications approach illuminates that authenticity trumps (pun intended) everything else because it embodies honesty, truth, and connection, even if *that* honesty, truth, and connection is not shared by millions of other people. It's human nature to want to be heard and helped. It creates a sense of being valued because it feels like you've been acknowledged. *You* matter. *Your* feelings have been validated. And Trump knew how to validate the feelings of his base.

"Those who truly lead are able to create a following of people who act not because they were swayed, but because they were inspired. For those who are inspired, the motivation to act is deeply personal."[xlv] These words from author and speaker Simon Sinek aptly capture what Trump was able to achieve.

Another challenge facing leaders who try to be authentic communicators is understanding the dynamic between being authentic and also being polished and articulate when they speak. This frequently surfaces during the filming of corporate videos. Many leaders I have worked with request multiple takes until there are no stumbles, no slip-ups, or no ums and ahs. Ironically, being willing to show these fallibilities only reinforces what employees want to see: that you are human and make mistakes, just like them. It's authenticity at its purest and very best.

Of course, that being said, no one wants to hear a constant string of "umms" and "ahhs" from a leader of any kind (business, political, military, etc.). Too much of this can erode confidence in the leader. Again, effective communication is more of an art than a science.

For those seeking to strengthen the authenticity of their communication, there are two foundational principles you must adopt. The first is practice your communication so that you're comfortable with the content; the second is to personalize your communication. Neither is profound, nor do they require external consultants or programs to implement. The only requirement is an unwavering commitment to caring about your words and the way you say them. If Harvard can teach it, it can be learned!

KEY TAKEAWAYS

- Leaders are often challenged with communicating authentically because it's difficult to get them to be vulnerable when they believe they must be perceived by others in a certain way.
- Authenticity has the capacity to help create the strongest possible connections with others when you can communicate in a very personal and "imperfect" way. It's about showing your humanity and that you are the same as everyone else — fallible, not flawless.
- Crises create especially challenging times to communicate with authenticity because of time pressures, lack of all the information desired to make informed comments, and possible legal exposure, but powerful, compelling, and authentic communications are still possible in these situations.
- Poorly managed crisis communications can result in a negative impact on an organization's reputation, employee morale, and financial performance.
- Authenticity can be learned with self-reflection, self-awareness, and feedback from others.

Part Four

Bringing It All Together

THE COMMUNICATION CHALLENGES

"The most important thing in communication is
hearing what isn't said"

— *Peter Drucker*

To be a truly impactful and powerful communicator, you must understand the challenges you will face. Only with this understanding will you be in a position to overcome them. While Drucker captures one underestimated challenge — non-verbal communication — what follows is a list of the other key challenges to be aware of.

TIME IS OF THE ESSENCE

Time is a challenge for all of us, and leaders have unique demands on their time. Nitin Nohria, dean of Harvard Business School, and Business School professor Michael Porter tracked the daily activities of CEOs at twenty-seven billion-dollar companies for thirteen weeks to discover their time-management practices.[xlvi]

Porter says, "Their life is endless meetings and a barrage of email. In a workshop we do with newly appointed CEOs, many say they are overwhelmed by managing the job. They say, 'I used to have a big job, but in the job of CEO, the demands on my time seem to have grown 100-fold. Everybody wants a piece of my time.'"

On average, CEOs spend 43% of their time on activities that furthered their agendas, while 36% is spent in a reactive mode, handling issues as they unfold. Nohria and Porter also found that CEOs attend an average of thirty-seven meetings each week, consuming 72% of their total work time, with another 24% of their time consumed by email.

Considering this one study alone, it appears that leaders just don't have the time to prepare for communications or to refine their skills. But this is one place where you cannot accept the status quo. The fact is, you are always communicating, even when you don't realize you are. And another fact is that employees hang on your every word. That puts you in a bind of competing forces.

Consciously and unconsciously, inferences and assumptions are constantly being made about what you say as employees form their own ongoing narrative about the world around them. So even with off-the-cuff comments, pause even after the fact, to reflect and consider how they might have landed. This is extraordinarily challenging because as humans our default is to respond immediately when someone speaks to us. This makes the "pause and reflect" strategy very challenging to deploy.

Whenever you can, set aside time to think about and plan your communications. Without this, you risk compromising consistency, transparency, and authenticity. It's nearly impossible to be consistent when you don't think about what has been said previously on a given topic or what you may be communicating in the days, weeks, or months to follow.

YOUR PAST, THE PRESENT

One of the hidden communication challenges is part and parcel of our upbringing: social conditioning. In her best-selling book *Lean In*, Sheryl Sandberg approaches communication from this more sociological perspective. She discusses the impact of being conditioned to speak "appropriately" while we are growing up, and in so doing, losing something in authenticity (and, I would add, transparency) when we are adults. I think she's spot on.

Sandberg says, "This reticence causes and perpetuates all kinds of problems: uncomfortable issues that never get addressed, resentment that builds, unfit managers who get promoted rather than fired, and on and on."[xlvii]

It is against this backdrop, I believe, that popular workplace colloquialisms such as "Why don't we discuss the elephant in the room?" or "Are we going to open the kimono?" were born. I mean seriously, how many elephants have you ever seen in a meeting room? As for your kimono, can we just keep it closed please? We use these and many phrases like them because we are afraid of being vulnerable and just telling it like it is.

What we must fight against when it comes to social conditioning is its negative impact on our ability to be vulnerable, a key driver of authenticity. In many circumstances, leaders find it difficult to be vulnerable, and as a result, colloquialisms make their way into conversation.

Others will argue that using phrases like these are a sign that we are trying to discuss sensitive matters, and I understand that. But as a leader, I am expecting more from you, and I guarantee others are as well. Just take it one step further and say: "I think we need to discuss something sensitive that I know is on everyone's mind," rather than speaking of elephants and kimonos.

FREE YOUR EGO

Why do some leaders find it so challenging to be vulnerable? In part, it stems from their belief that leaders must have all the answers. In their minds, intellect and competence enabled them to rise to a position of leadership and so they believe this must be demonstrated time and again lest someone think they are not fit for the role. Having the answers, it is believed, will lead others to see them as competent, and if that is achieved, then they are a "successful" leader and trust will follow. The downside of this way of thinking is that it overemphasizes the impact of competence.

While there's little doubt that employees want to view their leader as competent, they also want to see themselves in their leaders. They want to see a person they can relate to and who has similar experiences to theirs. When leaders display vulnerability, it shows them as human, the most obvious trait they share with employees. Vulnerability invites others into a more intimate relationship: it's an invitation to connect on a different, deeper, and more meaningful level.

A leader's ability to relate to others also sharply increases when employees experience someone as "just like them." In essence, vulnerability promotes connection, because it conveys a high level of trust.

Harvard Business Review hailed this as "a ground-breaking, paradigm-shattering idea," one of the most influential business ideas of the decade — emotional intelligence. In his 1996 book of the same name, author and psychologist Daniel Goleman suggested that EI (or emotional intelligence quotient) might actually be more important than IQ (which can be translated as "competence"). "EI trumps IQ in 'soft' domains, where intellect matters relatively little for success," said Goleman in a follow-up paper years later.[xlviii]

The number of leaders I've seen display some level of vulnerability can be counted on one hand. To be honest, in my entire career I have heard the following sentence exactly once from a leader: "I don't know, that's a good question." And when that elusive phrase crossed the lips of one of the most astute people I have ever worked with (who was the CEO of a large organization), there was an almost palpable pause in the room.

His disarming honesty and willingness to show some vulnerability (by not having an answer) seemed to shell-shock those around him. Their reactions were subtle, but I could tell from the expressions on their faces and the silence that ensued that this was a memorable moment.

This CEO also managed to deliver a double whammy with his comment, because while he was being vulnerable ("I don't know"), he was simultaneously being complimentary to another executive, one of his direct reports. In front of a room of that executive's peers, he was complimentary about the value of the question ("That's a good question"). There was no defensiveness, something I have frequently witnessed in situations like this. It usually comes out in an exasperated response which, without actually saying these words, is akin to "Why on earth would you ask such a *&%#@* stupid question?" This was the opposite — pure, unadulterated vulnerability.

MEN AND WOMEN CAN BE FROM THE SAME PLANET

What about gender? This is a variable that is closely related to social conditioning. From a very early age, we are taught about the ways boys and girls are supposed to speak. As we mature and grow older, these suggestions become deeply embedded in our personalities. We know from an abundance of research that men and women communicate differently. These differences are important to be mindful of, as they directly impact how effective our communication will be.

These are generalizations of course, but given women's higher EI, communication from them is often marked by active listening. They won't hold back from asking insightful questions or challenging a position. In my experience, they can be more patient than male leaders and are inclined to gather as much information as they can to try and understand fully what they are being told rather than immediately defaulting to the problem-solving phase that men tend to favour. Yet another reminder of the importance of context — and this is prime example where women tend to seek more of it.

Men's tendency is to communicate for a purpose (a.k.a. wanting to solve a problem). Frequently, responses are focused on the immediate resolution of a perceived problem. This manifests itself through a series of probing questions.

Communication, therefore, can be much more a means to an end for men versus an opportunity that women often pursue to connect, listen, and learn, which are the very things that will provide more impactful communication, deepen a connection, and help build trust.

John Gray, in his New York Times best-selling book *Men are from Mars, Women are from Venus*, says, "Either a man completely ignores [a woman] when she speaks to him, or he listens for a few beats, assesses what is bothering her, and then proudly puts on his Mr. Fix-It cap and offers her a solution to make her feel better."[xlix]

Although Gray's book is focused on communication between men and women in a romantic context, the essence of men moving immediately to action instead of just acknowledging and listening is also a familiar experience in the workplace. Yes, it's accurate to say that in many cases employees do want their leaders to solve problems. It's also accurate to suggest that at other times, they just want a supportive ear. It's incumbent on you to know what employees need and when. This is a "watch out" for male leaders and something they need to be conscious of when they approach communications.

According to Richard Drobnick, personally trained and licensed by John Gray, "[a woman] sees conversation as an act of sharing. She's looking for someone to listen and understand what she's feeling."

On the surface, it is easy to see how this kind of approach would lend itself more easily to transparent and authentic communication. Think of Oprah. It also explains why there is a pervasive view that women tend to be much stronger in the area of "soft skills" in leadership. One body of evidence to support this notion comes from the Hay Group who surveyed 55,000 professionals at all levels across ninety countries. One of their conclusions was that "women more effectively employ the emotional and social competencies correlated with effective leadership and management than men."[l]

BEYOND THE BROKEN TELEPHONE

If we turn our attention to cultural norms, here is another tricky area of communication where trust can be easily forged, or easily broken.

According a Harvard Business Review article, "Managing Multicultural Teams":

> The first difference is *direct versus indirect communication*. Some cultures are very direct and explicit in their communication, while others are more indirect and ask questions rather than pointing our problems. This difference can cause conflict because, at the extreme, the direct style may be considered offensive by some, while the indirect style may be perceived as unproductive and passive-aggressive in team interactions.[li]

Get it right, and it can be very powerful. Get it wrong, and the telephone might not just be broken but downright irreparable!

In a study conducted by Accenture on the chief factors causing problems between onshore and offshore workers, 76% of the nearly 200 senior-level executives interviewed cited differing communications styles.[lii] This is especially important to note for leaders who work across multiple geographic boundaries.

Working in global organizations, I have witnessed the challenge of successfully navigating different cultures firsthand. At times, the stakes are low and can make for educational, even lighthearted moments, like the time a new British CEO I was working with told me to meet him at the "lift" to go to a meeting we were headed to. A lift? I decided to wait for him to emerge from his office in a not-so-subtle manner so that I could walk with him to find out what this mysterious "lift" was. Lo and behold, it was the elevator!

But more often than not, the stakes are much higher and cultural missteps can lead to significant reputational damage, negatively impact a professional relationship, and erode trust.

When considering cross-cultural sensitivity and communication, consider the following analogies to add an extra layer of insight. They come from Brian Schroeder, Head of Culture and Communication at Microsoft.

Fish in a bowl: Just as fish swim in the water and are not aware of the nature of that water, we human beings, depending on the opportunities that we have had or have taken, may or may not be aware of the reality or the air outside our own bowl.

Onion: Each one of us, through our upbringing, education, work, and experiences in life, are layered beings.

Sunglasses: Culture enables us to frame issues. We look at the world according to the tint or the colour of the lenses that we wear. But as professionals, we have a responsibility toward our organizations to ensure we have the right lenses.

Iceberg: Just as a larger part of the iceberg is under water, there are a lot of things happening in any interaction that are below the surface. We have to make an effort to see not only what is above the surface, but also what is below.

The "iceberg" or nonverbal part of communication can exacerbate an already challenging interaction if you aren't cautious. My advice? Do your homework. There are so many diverse views on body language and what each gesture may or may not signal in each culture and country. I've included the key categories below that you should consider delving into further:

- Hand gestures
- Eye contact
- Proximity (physical space between you and another person)
- Greetings
- Body movement
- Posture
- Facial expressions

KEY TAKEAWAYS

- To be an effective communicator and understand how the Trust Trifecta can be compromised, you must understand the Communication Challenges.
- Intentionally set aside time to review planned communications. Considering and applying feedback on your communication style is critical if you want to see an improvement.
- Understanding your past (i.e., social conditioning) and the impact of it on your communication style is one challenge you should address. You must also consider this factor when others communicate with you.
- Generally speaking, men and women communicate differently. Understanding and appreciating these differences will help you become a stronger and more effective communicator.
- There are so many different cultural considerations to account for in communication that you should make the time to learn about the key differences, especially if you work in a global organization and have colleagues from other countries. Remember, different doesn't mean better or worse, it just means different!

THE COMMUNICATION MUST-HAVES

"Life is really simple, but we insist on making it complicated."

— *Confucius*

As with many things in life, people tend to complicate effective communication. True, you need to be thoughtful about what and how things are said, but at the same time, you should avoid overthinking things. After all, that's what lies at the heart of authenticity. What's important to appreciate is that powerful and impactful communication is a fine balance of intentions, skills, and commitment. There are many contributing factors to strong and poor communication, so being thoughtful is absolutely critical.

Thinking about how you like to be engaged by others and how that makes you feel is a good barometer to begin with. Modifying your style and trying out different approaches will also provide you with feedback and insight into how your communication is received by others. As Peter Drucker once said: "Everything measured, improves."[liii]

The Trust Trifecta concept is straightforward enough, but your communication strategy becomes more complex when you consider other "must-haves." Luckily, these are also readily learnable.

On the following pages are my communication must-haves. Integrating these into your approach will help to reinforce and strengthen your ability to build trust with your words.

Practice, Practice, Practice: Just as world-class athletes practice on an ongoing basis so that they are "play ready" for important games and tournaments, leaders need to invest the required time to practice being a world-class communicator. We have already established that free time is a rare commodity for leaders, so being structured about this will be necessary. It seems obvious, but if you ask executives how much time they spend reviewing and internalizing messages they want to communicate, the answer is likely "not much." Yes, they might bring in a coach for a large presentation or an important meeting, but after the "tips 'n tricks" have been learned, many leaders fail to spend time before each interaction thinking about how they will communicate.

You need to take a moment to prepare by asking yourself: What is the purpose of this specific communication? Is it to inform? Persuade? Influence? Recommend? Provide feedback? Just listen? What is it about this specific audience that I should consider? What are they needing to hear from me?

Thinking about and being clear about your purpose will help inform and shape your communications approach.

At the end of the day, spending time with your content and rehearsing how you want to share it is the most important driver in helping you to be more authentic. Doing so will enable you to come across as less scripted and help you connect more powerfully with those you are speaking with.

In essence, the more comfortable you are with your content, the more comfortable you will appear when delivering it.

Personalize Your Communication: As much as you should make it about the audience (remember, it's not about you!), sharing personal anecdotes and insights can actually help you reinforce that your focus is on the audience. By revealing something personal, you build a connection. Many times, leaders will rely on facts and stats in their communications to bolster the credibility of what they are saying. There is value in this approach, but this value can be substantially increased by using that data and connecting it to something personal.

As Stacey Snider, former President of DreamWorks said, "The best stories lead from the heart, not the mind."

Use Body Language: Comprising a set of non-verbal cues that includes posture and gestures, body language has a significant impact on how your communication is received. Leaning forward, tilting your head in the direction of someone you are speaking to, and making eye contact are all important. Gesturing is closely linked to speech, so using it while we talk can actually enhance our thinking.

Whenever I encourage executives and others to incorporate gestures into their delivery, I consistently find that their verbal content improves. Experiment with this and you'll find that the physical act of gesturing helps you form clearer thoughts and speak in tighter sentences with more declarative language. Again, this is more art than science, so find gestures that work for you and your style of delivery so they come across as natural versus forced.

Watch Your Cadence: One of the most common mistakes people make when communicating is speaking too fast. This is particularly true when delivering a presentation or a speech. People get nervous. The best antidote to talking fast is controlling and slowing your breathing. You need to practice this as it doesn't come naturally for most. The more you practice, the more comfortable with the content and the less nervous you will be. The less nervous you are, the slower you will speak. I promise.

Much has been written about cadence especially when it comes to some of the greatest orators of our time. John F. Kennedy (JFK) is said to have talked very fast. In fact, Kennedy made it into the Guinness Book of World Records for his rate of speaking. "During a speech in 1961, he spoke 327 words in just one minute. That's about 3 times faster than the normal conversation rate."[liv]

During his inaugural address, however, he slowed down to a remarkable 96.5 words per minute, the slowest rate in the past sixty years of inauguration speeches. Proficient at pacing, JFK had a keen sense of how to use language to get the audience both impassioned and focused, and measured each word to emphasize the meaning of his message.

Use Intonation: As with pacing, varying your level of intonation can also be very effective at emphasizing certain points. Be selective though: the last thing an audience (whether of one or one hundred) wants to hear is a verbal symphony coming from your mouth — it will only serve as a distraction. One common habit is "upspeak," the tendency to raise the pitch of one's voice at the end of a sentence. This is most noticeable during presentations in my experience.

While there are fierce debates on the existence and origin of "upspeak," as well as views that women tend to do this more than men, here is my view: Whether you are male or female, raising your voice to a higher pitch at the end of a sentence (in the absence of asking a question) conveys a lack of confidence in what you are saying. It comes across as if you are hedging or reluctant, and as a result, creates a sense that you doubt what you're saying. If you appear to not trust your own words, how can you possibly expect others to trust them?

Avoid Technical Language: For anyone who has specialized knowledge of a topic, avoiding technical language when discussing it can be very difficult. Yet using this type of language when trying to connect with non-technical people only serves to distract, or worse, bore people: they will tune out since they have no idea what you are saying. Remember, we want to make it *easy* for people to understand, and therefore connect with, what we are saying. The goal isn't just sharing information, but making a connection in order to build trust.

Covet Clarity: By keeping things simple, you will vastly improve the clarity of thought which is the cornerstone of powerful communication. If you are not absolutely clear on what you are saying, then how can you reasonably expect others to understand it? This is part and parcel of why you should avoid technical language, but even more important is ensuring your ideas come across clearly. Herb Kelleher, the longest-serving CEO of Southwest Airlines, once told someone, "I can teach you the secret to running this airline in thirty seconds. This is it: 'We are THE low-cost airline. Once you understand that fact, you can make any decision about this company's future as well as I can.'"[lv] Pretty simple, no?

Simplicity breeds clarity. One need only consider political campaigns to see how much weight is given to simplicity. The directive is to always "keep it simple." Again, that's exactly what Trump did with his words that resulted in a key takeaway for his supporters: "He understands what I'm afraid of and what I need. He also shares those same fears. If I support him, he will solve my problems."

Be Crisp: The ability to succinctly and crisply communicate your message will help drive clarity and simplicity. And the more clear and simple your message is, the better chance you have of communicating it in a crisp manner.

Once again, if you look to politics, you will see the epitome of "message discipline" at play. Strategists, pollsters, and communication advisors pore over data and insights to help them develop the messages that will resonate with voters.

Here is *Guardian* writer David Smith's take on Trump's key message of "Make America Great Again":

In four words it captured both pessimism and optimism, both fear and hope. The slogan harks back to a supposed golden age of greatness – the 1950s, perhaps, or the 1980s – and implies that it has been lost but then promises to restore it. It went straight to the gut, unlike rival Hillary Clinton's website manifesto and more nuanced proposals. It was an appeal to the heart, not the head, in a country where patriotism should never be underestimated.[lvi]

Another important consideration when it comes to messaging is ensuring that you don't have *too many* messages. People tend to remember two to three key takeaways from speeches, remarks, and presentations, so build a tight and focused story for the best results.

Ask Questions: Remember that communication is a two-way dialogue. The best way to recognize this is to ask questions. There are multiple reasons to ask questions and doing so can create tremendous value for you as a communicator. Think of a presentation setting. If you are presenting and suddenly stop to ask the audience a question, you are creating a moment of engagement and conversation by inviting the audience into the dialogue. If you are in a company meeting, asking questions can help you determine how much information the audience has retained from what you've been saying. It can help you understand whether they agree or disagree (by a simple show of hands or by using handheld technology where the audience answers questions in real time).

As a speaker in either setting, you can then use the audience input to reinforce a specific point or key message you want to convey or take that feedback and lean into a new direction with your communication.

A last word on asking questions: In the only US presidential debate between Ronald Reagan and Jimmy Carter, Reagan could have cited innumerable statistics demonstrating the sluggishness of the economy. Instead, he posed a simple request that allowed voters to test their satisfaction with the incumbent for themselves: "Before you vote, ask yourself if you are better off today than you were four years ago."

Like other aspects of communications, many of these fundamentals have been studied and measured. Quantified Communications, a Texas-based firm, used a proprietary communication analytics platform to measure the communication skills of CEOs at some of the largest companies in the US to identify who was the most authentic. What did they find?

Compared to the average leader in the company's analysis, they found that the twenty most authentic CEOs stood out in several ways:

- Their visual delivery (body language, gestures, eye contact) was 34% more effective.
- The most authentic CEOs used significantly more trustworthy language than average.
- Their messages were 29% clearer.[lvii]

Use Visuals: You know the age-old adage — a picture is worth a thousand words. Strong presenters appreciate this and will often only include an image on screen and just speak to it rather than fill the slide with excessive text. Visuals are especially impactful at the opening of a presentation because they set the stage. They can also be effective as a summary slide to close a presentation, leaving the audience with a lasting image that ideally summarizes the key message(s).

Know your audience: The best communicators spend time thinking about what the audience needs to hear from them before they start communicating. In doing so, they inherently understand that their purpose isn't being just a channel for message delivery, but a dynamic touchpoint and powerful connection that can create an impact. They will tailor their message accordingly because they will consider the emotion and intentions behind the content they are communicating.

One of the best questions you can ask yourself before most interactions is: What do I want this person (or persons) feeling after our interaction concludes? This will help shape not only your message but also how you deliver that message.

KEY TAKEAWAYS

- It's not enough to simply adhere to the fundamentals of the Trust Trifecta: there are many other communication must-haves that are essential to account for that will complement your ability to apply the principles of consistency, transparency, and authenticity.
- The most impactful way to strengthen your communication skills is through practice. Schedule time in your calendar to spend with your content. There will be an immediate payoff of confidence and comfort.
- By personalizing your communication, you create an additional opportunity for connection with the audience. Share something personal or an anecdote the audience can relate to.

- So much is said through non-verbal communication. You need to be aware of and utilize the different aspects of body language. Whether it's your eye contact or head and hand movement, be aware of how you are coming across.

- Many people have a tendency to speak too quickly when communicating, especially when dealing with difficult subject matter (so they can get it over with) or during crises (because of the additional pressure). Be conscious of this when communicating, particularly during presentations.

- As all good storytellers know, using your voice with varying intonation can be highly effective. You might speak loudly perhaps when asking a question of the audience and use another pitch when emphasizing an important point. And remember to watch out for and correct "upspeak," the tendency to elevate the pitch of your voice at the end of a sentence.

- Technical language should be avoided, unless, of course, it's in a technical briefing. This is a particular challenge for those leaders with specialized knowledge.

THAT'S A WRAP

"Every time you have to speak, you are
auditioning for leadership."

— *James Hume*

The interrelationship between leadership and communication is clear. Strong, impactful leadership demands strong, impactful communication skills. These are essential if you want to build trust. And make no mistake: the stakes are high.

David Solomon was appointed CEO of Goldman Sachs in 2018. About six months later, he was speaking to a group of students at his alma mater and shared his take on communication and connection. "How you communicate with other people, how you interact with other people, how you express yourself will have a huge impact on your success," said Solomon.[lviii]

Complexity in the workplace is growing. Impacted by globalization, regulation and transformation, mergers and acquisitions, strategic alliances, and new workforce models, effective leadership communication is a critical skill more than ever before. Employees are relying on leaders to help them make sense of the fast-changing world around them. But taking up the commitment to develop, refine, and strengthen this skill in yourself and others is up to you.

Surprisingly, many of the world's top-ranked business schools do not have stand-alone courses in, or indeed any focus on, the study of leadership communication.

At best, this is ironic given the fact that one of the most important accountabilities of a leader is to help employees and other stakeholders make sense of their organizations, their strategies, their decisions, their activities, and their direction. At worst, it's a sign that the impact of communication in terms of employee engagement and business performance is not well understood or accepted. More than anything though, it's surprising given how much research has been done on the leadership skills that are most important for success.

One example of such research is a study by Jack Zenger and Joseph Folkman of more than 330,000 bosses, peers, and subordinates that came up with a ranking of the leadership skills that are most important for success.

Number one was "[inspiring] and [motivating] others," notable not because of its predictable place in the ranking, but because demonstrating this skill rests largely on one's ability to effectively use another top-ranked skill: "[communicating] powerfully and prolifically" (ranked number five).[lix]

In other words, in order to motivate and inspire others and mobilize them around a vision, for example, one needs to articulate that vision in a meaningful and consistent manner. This is the only way others will follow you. Remember, followership, after all, is the necessary goal of every leader. This concept is embedded into each of us from the earliest age. Remember the phrase "follow the leader"?

But how does one engender followership? Why do some people choose to stick with you and deliver their best for you time and again? How do you influence people to believe in you enough that they decide to put their faith in you to make significant decisions on their behalf? How do you cultivate a following so strong that others will abandon long-held views about a subject because you don't share the same views?

It goes without saying — although here I am saying it — that people buy from people they trust. They buy goods and services, but also the words that are spoken and how those words are delivered. People want to work for people they trust.

As Jamie Dimon, JPMorgan Chase & Co. CEO, put it this way: "It's not necessarily how smart [leaders] are, or charismatic they are, not how hard they work. It's whether people want to work with them and for them."[lx] Therefore, if you are a leader who has direct reports follow you to your next role, even if it means leaving the organization to follow you, that's pretty strong evidence of Dimon's point. Alison Davis clearly grasped this point.

Enacting a strategy for impactful communication isn't straightforward. Done well, it is the perfect storm of many considerations coming into play and working harmoniously together. Because it's an art and not a science, it's not enough to just be consistent, transparent, and authentic in your communications without also considering tone, body language, clarity, and a host of other communication fundamentals.

Think of how many times you've walked away from a meeting or presentation where you were blown away by how amazing the speaker was. They were dynamic. Energetic. Articulate. And yet, a week later, do you remember the takeaway from their presentation? Would you trust them to make decisions on your behalf that could affect your life in a significant way today and in the future? The relationship you ought to seek with employees should extend far beyond a one-off, highly rated presentation or speech. This is because you inevitably ask so much more from employees than that perfectly timed, finely intonated, effectively hand-gestured presenter does.

Leaders ask employees to change their priorities so that they line up with what the leader believes they should be. A leader asks employees to stretch and strive beyond their annual goals in order to deliver higher performance. Some leaders may ask employees to stay late, work weekends, move their families across the world to take on a role, or assume responsibilities that are far outside of the employee's job description.

As a leader, to have employees not just accept these asks but embrace them with passion, dedication, and diligence means you will need to have established a strong connection. Because when that connection exists, trust can flourish and these asks will barely register on an employee's radar. Sure, employees realize they are working longer hours, or working harder during the hours they are working, but because you the leader have asked and they trust you, they take it on without a second thought. That's the power of trust. That's how you move both people and organizations.

EVERYONE LOVES STORIES

Powerful and compelling communication begins with understanding your audience and your objective in speaking with that audience. It ends with you delivering that message authentically, transparently, and consistently such that the audience leaves *feeling* something versus having only heard something. Human beings are emotional by nature. We want to have experiences, not just have data shared with us. We crave hearing stories — creative, exciting, and memorable stories — and we learn to be entranced by stories from a very young age.

The truth is, this need doesn't fade the older we get. The setting might change from a bedroom to a boardroom, but the desire to connect with others through stories, especially those that directly involve or affect us, are still of great interest to us and can be very powerful in influencing what we think and believe.

Chip and Dan Heath, authors of *Made to Stick*, reference the importance of emotion as one of their six principles to give ideas "stickiness": "We are wired to feel things for people, not for abstractions. Sometimes the hard part is finding the right emotions to harness. For instance, it's difficult to get teenagers to quit smoking by instilling in them a fear of the consequences, but it's easier to get them to quit by tapping into their resentment of the duplicity of Big Tobacco."[lxi]

There are countless examples of effective storytelling all around us. Consider presidential historian Jon Meacham's piece in *Vanity Fair* titled "The Once and Future King – Ten years on, Obama is still the master of America's story." Commenting on Obama's appearances during the 2018 midterms, Meacham writes, "Obama's personal answer to our current plight? Tell a better story. Insist on a more appealing counter-narrative. And follow his wife's counsel to go high when they — meaning Trump — go low. Obama believes in this rhetorical prescription to his core. And why shouldn't he? He mastered American politics by telling his own story, and Trump rose to office by telling a different one."[lxii]

The point is, as leaders, thinking about what an audience's needs are is a critical part of crafting a story that connects with them. Remember, it's not about you! It is an inherently selfless act and one that should challenge you to think about your objective with every interaction you have. Because with every interaction, you have an opportunity to motivate and mobilize, empower and engage. *Words matter.*

In his book *The Twelve Absolutes of Leadership*, Gary Burnison sums up this idea perfectly: "For a leader, communication is connection and inspiration — not just transmission of information. Yet it is often one of the most challenging leadership skills because it is so easy to say, but not so easy to do."[lxiii]

In *this* book, we reviewed some of the key communication challenges you will face: social conditioning; appreciating the differences between genders; cultural factors. We also discussed the importance of communications planning. For many business leaders, especially newer ones, they can often forget that leadership is more than setting a vision and playing in the strategy sandbox. They underestimate the profound impact their every word and action has on those around them. Think about and plan for effective communications. It is of paramount importance to success.

Speak less, listen more. Being a great communicator does not only mean being a great talker. Ask questions. Listen actively. We often find ourselves in the bad habit of thinking about how we are going to respond instead of just listening to the other person speaking. When we do this, we aren't truly engaged in the conversation. Leadership isn't about standing on a soapbox and shouting orders: it's about engaging people in dialogue, problem solving, planning, and execution. You often notice that the wisest people listen more and speak less. The less we talk, the more we can learn from those around us.

So remember:

1. Be authentic — Vulnerability is intoxicatingly powerful.
2. Be transparent — Say what you know and acknowledge what you don't.
3. Be consistent — It's not enough to say something: you must align your actions with your words.

The goal of impactful communication isn't to be perfect, it's to be impactful, to move and inspire people, and to foster trust. Reflect on what you've read on these pages. Try out the Trust Trifecta and see for yourself the impact it has on those around you. Then drop me a line and let me know how it went. I look forward to hearing from you.

"There is one thing that is common to every individual, relationship, team, family, organization, nation, economy, and civilization throughout the world — one thing which, if removed, will destroy the most powerful government, the most successful business, the most thriving economy, the most influential leadership, the strongest character, the deepest love. On the other hand, if developed and leveraged, that one thing has the potential to create unparalleled success and prosperity in every dimension of life. Yet it is the least understood, most neglected, and most underestimated possibility of our time. That one thing is trust."[lxiv]

— *Stephen Covey*

ENDNOTES

[i] Proof, CanTrust Index 2019. https://www.getproof.com/thinking/the-proof-cantrust-index/

[ii] Stephen Covey, Doug Conant. Harvard Business Review. 2016. Connection Between Employee Trust and Financial Performance

[iii] 2009/2010 Communication ROI Study™. Originally published by Watson Wyatt Worldwide Capitalizing on Effective Communication. How Courage, Innovation and Discipline Drive Business Results in Challenging Times

[iv] 2009/2010 Communication ROI Study™. Originally published by Watson Wyatt Worldwide Capitalizing on Effective Communication. How Courage, Innovation and Discipline Drive Business Results in Challenging Times

[v] 2002 Study. Watson Wyatt.

[vi] Trust that Binds: The Impact of Collective Felt Trust on Organizational Performance. Sabrina Deutsch-Salamon and Sandra L. Robinson. Journal of Applied Psychology 93(3):593-601

[vii] Winning. Jack Welch.

[viii] Oprah Winfrey. www.awakenthegreatnesswithin.com

[ix] LinkedIn study. www.business.linkedin.com

[x] Why People Believe in Their Leaders — or Not. MIT Sloan Management Review. Daniel Man Ming Chng, Tae-Yeol Kim, Brad Gilbreath, and Lynne Andersson.

[xi] David Solomon, CEO of Goldman Sachs. www.ca.finance.yahoo.com

[xii] Can Hillary overcome the "liar" factor? Politico. Steven Shepard.

https://poll.qu.edu/national/release-detail?ReleaseID=2274

[xiii] Hillary Clinton Asks Not for Trust, but for Faith in Her Competence. The New York Times. Michael Barbaro.

[xiv] When the Headline Is You. Jeff Ansell.

[xv] Edelman Trust Barometer. John Clinton.

[xvi] Inc Magazine – 2015 re: building alignment

[xvii] Gallup $Q^{12®}$ Meta-Analysis Rep. https://news.gallup.com

[xviii] According to Research. Here's the Single Key to Improving Employee Engagement. Joseph Folkman. www.forbes.com. May 2017.

[xix] Culture and Engagement: The Naked Organization. David Brown, Veronica Melian, Marc Solow, Sonny Chheng, Kathy Parker. www2.Deloitte.com

[xx] When the Headline is You. Jeff Ansell.

[xxi] How Leaders Speak: Essential Rules for Engaging and Inspiring Others. Jim Gray.

[xxii] The High Price Of A Low Performer: Managers Spend More Than a Full Day a Week Addressing Subpar Work. www.rh-us.mediaroom.com

[xxiii] https://www.vox.com/policy-and-politics/2020/3/28/21197995/coronavirus-stimulus-trump-inspector-general-wont-comply

[xxiv] https://www.npr.org/2020/02/28/810339057/lawmakers-press-administration-for-more-transparency-about-coronavirus-response

[xxv] https://slate.com/news-and-politics/2008

[xxvi] Transparency takes center stage in campaign for White House. www.startribune.com

[xxvii] Election 2016: The no-transparency campaign – CNNPolitics. https://www.cnn.com

[xxviii] The impact of positivity and transparency on trust in leaders and their perceived effectiveness. Steven M. Norman, Bruce J. Avolio, and Fred Luthans.

[xxix] Introductory Statement: Press Conference. https://www.ecb.europa.eu/press/pressconf/2019/html/ecb.is191212~c9e1a 6ab3e.en.html. Christine Lagarde.

[xxx] Dove Apologizes for Racially Insensitive Facebook Advertisement. https://www.nbcnews.com

[xxxi] United Airlines apologizes for "re-accommodating" a customer by literally dragging him off an overbooked plane. www.salon.com

[xxxii] United CEO says airline had to 're-accommodate' passenger, and the reaction was wild. www.cnbc.com

[xxxiii] Woman forcibly removed from Southwest Airlines plane after refusing to leave. www.theglobeandmail.com

[xxxiv] Top U.S. VW Exec Blames 'A Couple of Software Engineers' for Scandal. www.nbcnews.com

[xxxv] Dezenhall – Glass Jaw

[xxxvi] www.cnn.com

[xxxvii] Here are the scandals and other incidents that have sent Facebook's share price tanking in 2018. Salvador Rodriguez. www.cnbc.com

[xxxviii] www.jnj.com

[xxxix] When the Headline is You. Jeff Ansell.

[xl] The Truth About Authentic Leaders. Harvard Business School. Bill George.

[xli] The Authenticity Paradox Why feeling like a fake can be a sign of growth. Harvard Business Review. Herminia Ibarra.

[xlii] www.BBC.com

[xliii] How Trump won the election: volatility and a common touch. www.theguardian.com

[xliv] Made to Stick. Chip and Dan Heath.

[xlv] Start with Why. Simon Sinek.

[xlvi] www.fastcompany.com. August 3, 2018

[xlvii] Lean In. Sheryl Sandberg.

[xlviii] www.danielgolemna.info

[xlix] Men are from Mars, Women are from Venus. John Gray.

[l] Women Are Better at Using Soft Skills Crucial for..www.haygroup.com

[li] Managing Multicultural Teams. Harvard Business Review. Behfar, Brett, Kern. 2007.

[lii] Improved Cross-Cultural Communication Increases Global Sourcing Productivity, Accenture study Finds. www.newsroom.accenture.com

[liii] https://www.goodreads.com/quotes/172730-what-s-measured-improves

[liv] Your speech pace: guide to speeding and slowing down. www.medium.com

[lv] Nuts. Herb Kelleher.

[lvi] How Trump won the election: volatility and a common touch. www.theguardian.com

[lvii] www.quantifiedcommunications.com

[lviii] Goldman Sachs CEO reveals the valuable job skill he's finding 'less and less'. Julia LaRoche. www.ca.finance.yahoo.com

[lix] Top 10 Skills Every Great Leader Needs to Succeed. www.inc.com

[lx] JPMorgan CEO Jamie Dimon's most important advice to succeed in business — Be nice. Tae Kim. www.cnbc.com

[lxi] Made to Stick. Chip and Dan Heath.

[lxii] Jon Meacham's piece in Vanity Fair titled, 'The Once and Future King' – Ten years on, Obama is still the master of America's story'.

[lxiii] The Twelve Absolutes of Leadership. Gary Burnison.

[lxiv] The Speed of Trust. Stephen Covey.

ACKNOWLEDGEMENTS

When you do something as challenging as writing a book, it's definitely a team sport! I have many people to thank for their guidance, counsel, feedback, honesty, expertise, and support. This includes all the folks at Iguana, including Greg, Toby, Holly, Rachel, and Meghan. Early on in the process Derek Finkle of the Canadian Writer's Guild was very generous with his time and perspective, which was really valuable. Hilary Bain, Joanne Campbell, and Trish Krause, friends and colleagues who read an early draft and helped set me on the right path. John Capobianco and Sharene Herdman for being terrific partners throughout my career and for offering their views on this book. But none of this would have been possible without the idea for it, which came from my friend and mentor, Jeff Ansell. One of the sharpest communications people around, he was my earliest cheerleader, insisting that I had a concept I could work with. He read multiple early drafts and his feedback, candour, and motivation were invaluable. To all of you, my deepest and heartfelt gratitude.

CPSIA information can be obtained
at www.ICGtesting.com
Printed in the USA
BVHW081316180920
589008BV00002B/214